David Adam was born in Alnw
Vicar of Danby in North Yorksh
discovered the gift for writing prayers ... ...
His first book of these, *The Edge of Glory*, achieved immediate
popularity. He has since published several collections of prayers
and meditations based on the Celtic tradition. His books have
been translated into various languages, including Finnish and
German, and have appeared in American editions. Having
retired from being Vicar of Holy Island, where he had taken
many retreats and regularly taught school groups on prayer, David
now continues this work and his writing from Waren Mill in
Northumberland.

AIDAN, BEDE, CUTHBERT

Three inspirational saints

DAVID ADAM

Illustrations by
Monica Capoferri

First published in Great Britain in 2006

Society for Promoting Christian Knowledge
36 Causton Street
London SW1P 4ST
www.spckpublishing.co.uk

British Library Cataloguing-in-Publication Data
A catalogue record for this book is available from the British Library

ISBN 978-0-281-05773-3

Typeset by Graphicraft Limited, Hong Kong
First printed in the UK by CPI Bookmarque, Croydon, CR0 4TD
Subsequently digitally printed in Great Britain

Produced on paper from sustainable forests

To the Society of the Sacred Mission,
which gave me a great love for the saints

Contents

Chronology of Events

616 Aethelfrith's victory at Chester; he kills monks at prayer.
Edwin defeats Aethelfrith and becomes king of North-umbria.
Aethelfrith's children Eanfrith, Oswald, Oswy and Ebba flee to Dalriada.

627 Edwin baptized at York by Paulinus on Easter Day.

628 Birth of Benedict Biscop.

632 Edwin killed by Penda.

633 Eanfrith becomes king of Bernicia and Osric king of Deira.

634 Eanfrith and Osric both killed by Penda and Cadwalla.
Battle of Heavenfield. Oswald defeats Penda, kills Cadwalla and becomes ruler of Northumbria.

635 Aidan comes to Northumbria at Oswald's invitation and establishes a monastery on Lindisfarne.
Birth of Cuthbert.

642 Oswald killed in battle. Oswy succeeds to Bernicia and Oswin to Deira.

651 Oswin is murdered on the instructions of Oswy.
Aidan dies at Bamburgh on 31 August.
Cuthbert has a vision of angels taking Aidan to heaven. He enters the monastery at Melrose.

664 Synod of Whitby. Bishop Colman leaves for Iona then Ireland, taking some of Aidan's bones with him.

668 Theodore of Tarsus consecrated as Archbishop of Canterbury.

670 Oswy dies and is succeeded by Ecgfrith as king of North-umbria.

673 Birth of Bede.

674 St Peter's, Wearmouth founded by Benedict Biscop.

680 Bede enters the monastery at Wearmouth.

681 St Paul's monastery at Jarrow founded. Bede and Ceolfrith among its founding members.

685 Cuthbert is made bishop of Lindisfarne at York on Easter Day.

Dedication of St Paul's, Jarrow.

Ecgfrith killed in battle and Aldfrith succeeds him.

686 Plague year when Jarrow and Wearmouth are badly affected.

687 Death of Cuthbert on 20 March.

689 Death of Benedict Biscop.

692 Bede ordained deacon by Bishop John of Hexham.

703 Bede ordained priest by Bishop John.

716 Ceolfrith dies at Langres on his way to Rome.

721 Bede completes his prose *Life of Cuthbert*.

731 Bede completes his *History of the English Church and People*.

735 Death of Bede on Ascension Eve, 25 May.

Introduction

When Aidan died, Cuthbert was only sixteen. Though they never met, their lives touched each other. When Cuthbert died Bede was only twelve. Again they never met, but Bede was deeply influenced by both Cuthbert and Aidan. And through Bede's writings we discover how these lives had a lasting effect on each other. Now, 1,300 years later, I am aware of how I have been touched by the lives of Aidan, Bede and Cuthbert, and how they have helped to make me who I am.

One of the wonderful things about our lives is that they are interwoven with those of so many others. There are people who influence us greatly by their relationships, by their example or by their writings. Sometimes people have made our lives turn in a new direction, even if at the time we hardly noticed that it was happening. We all owe a great debt to so many people, those who taught us the faith as well as those who taught us to read and write. Sometimes people's prayers and resources have supported us without us ever knowing their presence. Lives touch sometimes by the physical contact of hands and at other times over centuries, through books and through story.

I was thinking such thoughts one day in 1959 as my fingers traced out the letters 'Hac sunt in fossa Baedae venerabilis ossa', on the dark blue marble slab in the Galilee Chapel of Durham Cathedral. My Latin ability was just enough to let me translate: 'Here in this tomb are the bones of the Venerable Bede.' As I traced the letters I looked up at a wall painting of Cuthbert dressed as a bishop and giving his blessing. I knew I would need every blessing I could get. I was aware of how Bede's life was influenced by Cuthbert and how in his turn Cuthbert was influenced by Aidan. These lives touched in time as they overlapped. I was aware that the same three men had deeply influenced my life, though many centuries separated us.

It was only five days before Christmas. In many ways I was quite unprepared. I had other things on my mind. On this day, 20 December 1959, I was preparing to be ordained deacon in the Church of England by the Right Reverend Maurice Harland, Bishop of Durham, before serving my first curacy in St Helen's Auckland with West Auckland, in the Durham diocese.

Six years before, I had felt that God was calling me to full-time ministry. Why me? I could understand his choice only in the terms of 1 Corinthians 1.27–29: 'God chose what is foolish in the world to shame the wise; God chose what is weak in the world to shame the strong; God chose what is low and despised in the world, things that are not, to reduce to nothing the things that are, so that no one might boast in the presence of God.'

In the 1950s I was working underground at the Shilbottle coal mine in North Northumberland, near my home town of Alnwick. If I hoped for anything it was to be a mining survey-or, though I had not at this point graduated from shovelling coal dust. I had only a tenuous link with the Church and I did not find its worship very exciting. Yet there was something, or Someone, disturbing my inner being. Whenever I was not arm wrestling with a young fellow worker or shovelling coal, I wrestled with God and his call.

Time and again I had the feeling of being called to work full time in the Church, a feeling that I ought to offer myself for ministry. I was only 17; in many ways I found the idea absurd and tried to hide from it. Yet in the silence of the mine, while I shovelled coal dust, the idea, the call, came again and again. I knew so little of the Church, though I had attended a church school as a junior and learnt much of the heroes of the Bible and of the northern saints. I was fortunate to have been taught at a time when heroes were still presented to us, as was the challenge to live heroically. Our heroes were not shown with feet of clay, they were to be looked up to and copied. I greatly admired the courage of Captain Scott and his battle against the elements. I visited the place where Grace Darling was buried at Bamburgh and thought of her heroic rescue of the shipwrecked. At junior school I learnt of the mighty heroes of the faith, as our headmaster loved telling stories from Bede's *Ecclesiastical History*. I was familiar with the places where Aidan had lived and worked. I could point out the places where Cuthbert had exercised his ministry.

My father was a lorry driver who spent a lot of time delivering concrete pipes in Northumberland and the Borders. He used to point out the sites of battles and places associated with saints to me as I sat in the cab of his lorry. It was my father who first showed me the view of Holy Island from the Great North Road and told me it was where Aidan and Cuthbert had lived. It always looked so mysterious to me. Later, when he was delivering to the island, he took me across the sands in his lorry. One after another we passed the posts marking the Pilgrim's Way. The Castle looked like a dream in the early morning light and I was aware of an extra brightness, a radiance natural to this tiny offshore isle. How all this led me towards ordination I am not sure, but the stories of the saints were part of my own searching and seeking. Now, to be ordained in Durham Cathedral, one of the finest buildings in the world, was a great bonus. Here was the tomb of Bede and the tomb of Cuthbert. I was standing in my hall of heroes.

Wearing the dog-collar for the first time, I was surprised how comfortable it was. I had put on cassock, surplice and stole in preparation for my ordination. My parents had bought the stole as an ordination gift. My mother had been a great strength, and was likely the main reason I was here. She was very shy and gentle and suffered greatly from asthma. Often bed bound, she had taken to saying Morning and Evening Prayer from the Book of Common Prayer daily. Each day as she prayed she remembered my calling. This day in Durham would have been very special for her, yet she had died five months earlier. I felt that if it were possible, she would be looking on with great joy. My father was proud to see me ordained but at the same time mystified by the whole affair. In fact, I was totally mystified myself!

As I looked back, I was grateful for the training I had received from the Society of the Sacred Mission at Kelham near Newark in Nottinghamshire. I can remember being attracted to it by a priest named John Christie. On a visit to my parish priest, Canon Eyton Lloyd, Christie described Kelham as 'the commando course of the Church of England'. To me, full of energy as I was and wanting to do something exciting, this sounded attractive. It would be good to be trained in a strong way with discipline and a definite purpose. I was so weak in the faith that I would need it. I had a deep desire to know more of God and to serve him. I liked the idea of being one of God's commandos, battling against the evils of the world.

Kelham's training was of a monastic style. You had to attend church seven times every day and the bell governed everything. The rapid journey from mine to monastery at the age of 18 came as a shock to my system, and for the first few weeks I was completely out of my depth: I could not find my way around the services. Yet the chapel, with the strong Christ on the cross and the Blessed Virgin looking like some powerful peasant, helped me to feel at home. I began to realize the importance of imagery and visual arts. I was reminded of the love and the power of God whenever I entered the chapel.

The emphasis at Kelham was on worshipping and knowing God rather than just talking about him. I learnt to live by the rules of poverty, chastity and obedience. I discovered the power of silence, for this was how we kept a large part of each day. As the founder had written, 'He who cannot keep silence is not content with God.' Silence began after the evening service of Compline; that was not too bad, as it was nearly ten o'clock and time for bed. But then it continued the next day, often until lunchtime, and that took some getting used to. During the silent meals we had a lector reading to us from some 'interesting' book or other. Yet silence became a natural part of my life. I learnt that you are happy to be still and quiet if you are there with your loved one, that you do not always need words. My relationship with my God was growing in the silence.

Because they were used continuously within the daily services, I learnt all the psalms by heart. And I mean heart, rather than mind, for I learnt them in worship. Psalm 119, or a good part of it, was the first psalm I learnt, as we said it every day. This was not meaningless repetition but a deepening of the words until each one vibrated with love and the power of God. It was like hitting a nail with a hammer, slowly driving deeper the content and the meaning of each psalm. At the same time it was a turning of the heart as well as the mind to God. Like Aidan and the early saints, soon I was able to say the psalms while travelling and without a book. I could share in the daily services of Kelham while I was on a train or in my father's lorry. In many ways this freed prayer from being an activity that only seemed to take place in buildings. I could pray alongside all of God's creation.

I was also introduced to the beauty of Gregorian chant, to plainsong and to antiphonal singing. Such music had been introduced into Northumbria in the time of Bede. I was fortunate to have as my tutor Brother Edwin, one of the leading exponents of plainsong. He travelled to other colleges to teach the art, but he was resident at Kelham. I discovered the gentle flow, the rise and fall of the notes, like the wind or the rise and fall of the sea. Such music is a form of meditation and a learning to abide in the presence. There were times when the words hardly mattered. What mattered was that I was there and God was there with me.

The rhythm of my whole life became much like that of the early saints of northern England. Time was spent in worship and study, or in manual labour. The silence allowed for experiments in various approaches to prayer and meditation. Over the five years I spent at Kelham I learnt various traditional ways of prayer. I learnt too, in the quiet of a side chapel with no one about, how to pray in cross vigil, that is with my arms outstretched to make the shape of a cross. I discovered that it was sometimes good to call upon God many times during the day or night, and at other times just to remain before him in silence. God wanted a relationship with me that was more than just words.

I learnt not only to pray to the glory of God but also to scrub out toilets, dig soil, shovel coal and mend electric lights – all to the glory of God. Of course, if you were doing it for God's glory it meant you could not skimp on the job or be careless about it. I was learning to live theology, not only to study it. It would be no use knowing all the right words and not personally knowing the God whom they were about. I was slowly learning to 'practise the presence of God' in all that I was doing. I owe a debt to Brother Lawrence, who talked of such a practice in the seventeenth century. He was greatly encouraging, for he said, 'Nor is it needful that you should have great things to do . . . We can do little things for God.' As I stood in Durham Cathedral on this cold winter's day I knew I owed the Society of the Sacred Mission more than I could ever say; through them I had learnt to do little things to God's glory.

Suddenly someone else came to mind: Mr Elliot, the headmaster of my junior school in Alnwick. At an early stage Mr Elliot took me under his wing and saw that I got the encouragement I needed. He understood that I came from a poor background and needed to grow in confidence. I remembered how he was a firm disciplinarian and how I had once received the strap every day for a week! But I also thought of his love for the stories of Bede and how he would delight in telling us of Aidan and Cuthbert, of Hilda and Caedmon. With Mr Elliot the tales of the saints would come alive and he would hold the attention of us all. He reminded us that these were real people who had lived in the area we were living in now. Through his teaching I discovered that saints were not plaster figures or confined to stained glass windows, but humans with passions and feelings like us.

My ordination was a kaleidoscope of many feelings. Here was the resting place of some of my most loved saints. In procession with my fellow ordinands, I walked from the Galilee Chapel at the west end of Durham Cathedral, containing the bones of Bede and the fresco of Cuthbert, towards the east end of the magnificent gothic building and the tomb of St Cuthbert. I had stood there earlier that morning in the Chapel of Nine Altars and looked at the simple carving that said CUTHBERTUS. No doubt Cuthbert would have been happier with the simplicity of this tomb than all the richness and pomp of the pre-Reformation shrine. Cuthbert had been called from watching sheep to be a shepherd within the Church; in my turn, I prayed there that I would be worthy of my calling to share in the care of God's people.

Now, as I processed down the cathedral with the choir singing, I could not help but think of some of the others who were buried here – or who at least had some of their mortal remains within the cathedral. An Old English poem composed soon after Cuthbert's uncorrupted body was translated to the cathedral in 1104 describes its 'breathtaking site' and lists the relics of the saints who have been brought there: not only the body of Cuthbert, but also the head of king Oswald, some of the bones of Aidan and those of Eadfrith, the writer of the Lindisfarne Gospels; not only Bede but also the abbot Boisil who taught Cuthbert when he was at Melrose. What a place for a patriotic Northumbrian to be ordained in. Would I ever be able to live up to my calling?

During the next few years I learnt a great deal. Not only did I learn the delight of visiting people in their homes, I learnt to share in their joys and their sorrows. More than once, when I thought I would 'take God' to someone I found he had been there long before me. I was meeting God in others and discovering his presence awaiting me in their homes. I was gaining far more from people than I thought I ever brought to them.

For the first year I was in 'digs' with a wonderful Durham family next to an old mill. John, the man of the house, offered to 'ride shotgun' for me when I told him I was to take services in a nearby parish. It was a village that the county had designated 'category D', meaning it was due for demolition. Fifty years on, it survives and is thriving. John told me, 'It's called Jam Jar City and it lies in Treacle Tin Valley.' I thought he was joking, but it was true. The nicknames had arisen because the old miners drank out of jam jars and made mugs for themselves out of treacle tins. In time I met some of these old men and they were great characters. While many authorities avoided condemned areas, the Church was there and was very much involved. The clergy were among the few who were accepted and invited into the homes of these people with trust and hope. Many a time a space was cleared at the end of a table so that we could share in the sacrament of Communion.

While at West Auckland I had the privilege of celebrating one of my early Communions in one of the oldest churches in England, the Saxon church of Escomb with its circular grave-yard that may have reflected the belief of earlier times in the encircling of God, that God is all around us and protects us. The circle was believed to keep the devil out because it was a symbol of God's protecion. Many of the stones for this church had been taken from a neighbouring Roman settlement. The barn-like building is believed to have been built in the seventh or eighth century and may have been an example of the type of church a nobleman had built on his estate, as Bede mentions in his writing of John of Beverley. A simple Saxon sundial is set in the south wall of the church and there is a stone marked with the sign of one of the Roman legions. It was wonderful to celebrate in a church which had such a great history and where worship had gone on for centuries. There really was a sense of the communion of saints.

While at West Auckland Denise and I married. God would teach me the wonders of his love through Denise, who loved me and whose love continues to enrich my life and astound me. We learn so much of the love of God through others. At the same time I was discovering the 'otherness' of another person. Denise is a mystery to me! We should never assume we fully know a person; there is always more to discover and to enjoy. The great 'Other' who is God comes to us in others and speaks to us through others. Our sensitivity to other people tells us about our awareness not only of them but also of God. Becoming aware of the other is to begin to experience the holy. God often comes to us 'in the stranger's guise'.

After West Auckland, I served a second curacy on a large housing estate in what was then the separate town of West Hartlepool. There were over 20,000 people and a church built on the edge of the estate. These were amazing days when children queued to get into the newly proposed Sunday school high up on the estate. No doubt they did not know what they were coming to! There were just two of us on the first Sunday, trying to cope with a crowd of over three hundred children! We eventually got better organized, and even though we lost many of these children immediately, we still ran two Sunday schools whose attendance topped two hundred between them. There was a thirst for attention and for someone to care, if not for learning. I was now beginning to struggle with only the prayer book as a resource, so I started writing simple prayers for the young people to use. At this stage I was greatly indebted to the Scottish theologian William Barclay and his prayers for young folk. He wrote prayers and commentaries on the Bible with the lay person in mind, so that they might come 'to know better their Bible, their God and their Saviour'. On the estate I also celebrated in a school to which I carried a little travelling altar: it was made of oak from an old pit tub and carved into its top were five crosses, symbols of the wounds of Christ. This little altar must have been like the ones that the early Christian priests carried around as they shared Communion with various groups over a wide area. While at Hartlepool I was able to take a service in St Hilda's church, where I celebrated the life of that great princess of the Church and the influence she had on such men as John of Beverley and Caedmon. The Headland area of Hartlepool is still proud of its connection with Hilda, who had a monastery there.

The first parish I had on my own was St Hilda's, Danby in North Yorkshire. It was situated over the hilltops from the village of Lastingham, famed for the saints Cedd and Chad. This was the country that Bede described as 'some high and remote hills, which seemed more suitable for the dens of robbers and haunts of wild beasts than for human habitation ... where formerly lived wild beasts or men who lived like wild beasts'. Someone must have done their work since he wrote, because in the main I found the people who lived on these moors an absolute joy. St Hilda's, Danby is in the deanery of Whitby and when the Church of England moved to synodical government I attended the second Synod of Whitby. The first time we met I asked for the minutes of the previous meeting, to be told that there were no such minutes, as there had been no previous meeting. I pointed out that there had been such a meeting in 664 and that Bede had recorded its minutes quite well in his *History*. I had the joy of celebrating the Eucharist in Whitby and in the crypt at Lastingham during my years at St Hilda's. I also looked after the church in Commondale; it was said that this was 'Colman's dale' and that this bishop of Lindisfarne had a cell there.

During this time my love for the Celtic saints and those of the north east of England continued to grow. I visited Durham, Holy Island and Jarrow. I began to look at the lives of Aidan, Bede and Cuthbert in greater depth. I started to explore the simplicity of Celtic prayer and the complexity of Celtic artwork. With a group mainly of teenagers I explored ways of writing prayers in the 'Celtic style'. We were discovering ways of enriching our prayer life. I wanted the young shepherd, who was no scholar, to be able to pray as he cared for sheep and to enjoy his time of prayer; I wanted the potential nurse to discover the power and peace of the presence of God in all her dealings. Church prayers were often just that, for church. We were seeking prayers that were at home in the home, that worked at work. Such prayers would enrich our church prayers, and in turn the church prayers would enrich our own personal praying.

My time with these young folk would have a great effect on my life. I started a prayer diary and wrote a prayer, usually in the Celtic style, each day. I thrilled to see the shepherd lad leading prayers in church. In the 1980s I started to lead retreats and to help to direct others in the way of prayer. My own inspiration often came from my ABC – from Aidan, Bede and Cuthbert.

I was present on Lindisfarne in 1987 to commemorate the 1,300th anniversary of Cuthbert's death – although strangely I was there not in March for Cuthbert's day but at the very end of August, for St Aidan's day. It was on 31 August that Aidan died at Bamburgh. The same night, Cuthbert saw angels descending to the earth and taking a holy soul up to heaven, and the next day he heard that Aidan had died. Cuthbert saw this as a sign and offered himself to the monastery of Melrose. On that very night, 1,300 years later, I felt that again I was being called to do something new, though what, I did not know. I walked out of the retreat house on Holy Island and made my way into the dark, asking two other residents for the weekend to come with me; if something happened I needed a witness or two.

Going into the dark was a symbol of where I stood. People often tell me that God has told them what to do, but I always seem to struggle to discover his will. This tme, however, I had a vision of my own. As soon as we left the few street lights behind I saw a shooting star, then another, and another. After foolishly counting nearly a hundred of them I gave up. I wanted to ask, had Cuthbert seen stars or angels? I knew the answer was yes, though he might have seen it differently! But the question is not one of 'either . . . or'; it demands the answer 'both and more'.

We need not choose between stars and angels, but we need to keep ourselves alert to the greater potential that is ever being presented to us. You might decide the night was full of stars; that is beautiful enough. I, though, decided that once again God was calling me to do something – but what?

Meanwhile, in 1989 I was made a canon of York, in the Minster built on the site where Paulinus baptized Hilda and Edwin, where Chad was bishop and Wilfrid built a stone church. It was here too that Archbishop Theodore consecrated Cuthbert as bishop in front of king Ecgfrith. Once again a 'cloud of witnesses' surrounded me. Here was the history of the Church in England all about me, and I was a living part of it. No wonder I felt overawed when made 'canon of York and prebend of Botevant' and led to my own stall within the Minster.

It was Archbishop William Temple who said, 'When I pray coincidences happen. When I do not pray they do not happen.' Well, I had at least experienced a coincidence in 1987, when I saw shooting stars on 31 August, the same night that Cuthbert in 651 had seen angels in the sky. But it took another two years to move me. It still came as a great surprise when in 1989 the Bishop of Newcastle offered me the parish of Holy Island. In a sense it filled me with fear. It was a place of my dreams and of pilgrimage; could I allow it to become the 'ordinary' place where I worked? I loved the North Yorkshire Moors where I lived and I was reluctant to move. It was a case of 'God calls and man stalls'. Though other people seemed to think it was right, I still had to be convinced. But Denise saw more clearly than I did, and she knew we must move on. Just after Easter 1990 we moved to the island.

We would spend the next 13 years on the Holy Island of Lindisfarne. When I was inducted I was presented with a stole on which were embroidered depictions of Aidan and Cuthbert and a large photo-facsimile of the Lindisfarne Gospels, the Gospel book which was such a great witness to the enrichment that Christianity brought to this land and to the way cultures cross-fertilized each other.

I would be asked to pray where Aidan had prayed, where prayer had been said for over 1,300 years. I would be expected to exercise pastoral care where Cuthbert had exercised his care, where he had given comfort and solace to those who came. People had always come here for healing and for forgiveness, for spiritual direction and for new hope. Now thousands of people came every year. I would meet pilgrims from all over the world, who had the same love for Aidan and Cuthbert as I had. Time and again I would lead services in celebration for the witness of the saints of northern England. My copies of Bede's *History* and his *Life of Cuthbert* would soon need replacing. The stories were becoming part of my daily life: they seemed to be part of the very air I breathed.

Bede paid a visit to Holy Island when he was writing his book on Cuthbert. One of his requests to the monks is that they would one day include him in the Book of Life – that is the Remembrance Book – and keep his memorial. No doubt they did this, but it would be lost along with much else during the Viking invasion, though there is a ninth-century copy of the Durham Confraternity Book in the British Library that contains Bede's name. While on the island I had the privilege of dedicating a new Memorial Book. It included the names of the saints of the north-east, along with those of islanders who had recently died. Bede's name was inscribed on 25 May, his memorial day. I had thus fulfilled his request, ensuring that his name was once again in the *Liber Vitae*, the Book of Life, on Holy Island.

When Denise and I left the island we went to live at Waren Mill, only about five miles from the island as the crow flies but fifteen miles by road. We now live in the parish of Bamburgh, where Aidan first came to be given the island of Lindisfarne by king Oswald. I see the rock of Bamburgh Castle almost every day when I go for my newspaper. Here Aidan celebrated Easter with Oswald and Oswald gave away his food and silver dish to the poor. I now worship in the church built on the site where Aidan died. I can look at the wooden beam that is supposedly the one he leant against at his death. Remembering that this is a place of angels as well as saints, I pray that I may continue to keep that vision, that I may know that there is more to this world than what I see. May I be aware of the deep mysteries that are all around us and rejoice in the great Other who is God.

I offer you here my ABC as a guide in expanding your spiritual awareness and deepening your love for God. Aidan, Bede and Cuthbert have much to teach us about vision; that is, about how we see life.

Exercises

1 'Look to the rock from which you were hewn and to the quarry from which you were dug' (Isaiah 51.1).

Seek to see in your life the lives that have touched yours and influenced you greatly. Rejoice where you can and seek to forgive where you need to forgive. Know that many people have made you who you are. Give thanks for those who gave you life and who sustained you in the early years. Remember your teachers and all who have inspired you. In acknowledging his debt to others, Bernard of Chartres, who died in 1130, wrote: 'We are like dwarfs on the shoulders of giants: we can see more than they can, and things further off, not because we are keener-sighted or physically distinguished, but because we are being carried high, and lifted up by their great size.'

Sometimes when I give thanks for my past I trace over a Celtic knotwork pattern. Every time the pattern rises I give thanks for some good event in my life. When the line goes under another I seek forgiveness for some experience or person of the past. Above all this I acknowledge that the pattern is endless – I am still here through all the ups and downs, through all the encounters for good or bad – and life is eternal.

2 Vision is about seeing. How you look at life makes you the sort of person that you are. Read the story of Jacob from Genesis 28.10–17.

Picture the situation. Visualize Jacob alone, outdoors and under the stars. Share in his vision of the angels descending and ascending. Listen to God speaking. Hear God saying to you, 'I am with you and will keep you wherever you go . . . I will not leave you.'

Ask yourself: 'Have I woken out of sleep?' Are your eyes still closed to the wonderful mysteries of life that are always about you? Can you say with Jacob, 'Surely the Lord is in this place' – or do you not know it?

Say each day, 'How awesome is this place! This is none other than the house of God, and this is the gate of heaven' (Genesis 28.17).

You may like to think over the words of the poet Francis Thompson:

> The angels keep their ancient places; –
> Turn but a stone, start a wing!
> 'Tis ye, 'tis your estranged faces,
> That miss the many splendoured thing.
> (From the poem 'The Kingdom of God')

3 Pray:

> God, open my eyes to the beauty of your world:
> to the wonders and mystery of creation:

to your presence and to your power.
Open my heart to the love of others:
to their goodness and their grace:
to the great love that you have for me.

AIDAN

Aidan and the open door

Aidan could hardly believe what he had heard. Corman and the little group of monks who had gone with him had returned to Iona in 634, only a short while after leaving with the blessing of the community. At their departure there had been great rejoicing that an earthly kingdom wanted to know of the kingdom of heaven. Oswald, the new king of Northumbria, had spent some time on Iona in exile. He had become a Christian and hoped that one day he might share in the bringing of Christianity to Northumbria. It was said that, earlier that year, before his decisive battle at Heavenfield near Hexham and the Roman Wall in Northumberland, Oswald had a vision of St Columba. The saint had reminded him of words from the Old Testament book of Joshua at the river Jordan: 'Be strong and of good courage. Behold, I shall be with you. Be determined and confident, for you will be leader of these people as they occupy the land.' And he added, 'March out this following night from your camp to battle, for on this occasion the Lord has granted that your foes shall be put to flight.'

Oswald ordered a cross to be made from two saplings and set it up before his troops set out to fight, holding it with his own hands while it was made secure in the ground. This was the first mention of a cross being raised in Northumbria. When this was done he summoned his army with a loud shout, saying, 'Let us all kneel and ask the true God, the Almighty, of his mercy to protect us from the arrogant savagery of our enemies, since he knows we fight in a just cause to save our nation.' Like the great emperor Constantine who won a battle after seeing the sign of the cross, Oswald marched out hoping for victory.

The attack before dawn gave Oswald the element of surprise and caught the enemy off guard. Penda of Mercia and Cadwallon of Gwynedd were defeated, and Cadwallon was killed. Oswald had regained the kingdom of Northumbria that his father Aethelfrith had ruled before his death at the hands of Edwin, prince of Deira. As soon as he was in control of the kingdom and had established his stronghold in Bamburgh, he sent to Iona for teachers and preachers, that his people might be educated and hear the gospel of Christ. Just as the monks of Iona had reached out to the Pictish kingdoms, they now had a great opportunity to reach out to the land of the Angles. Here was a mighty kingdom, stretching from the Forth to the Humber, waiting to be won for Christ. Here was a wonderful chance to bring the love of God to bear on a warlike people. It would be a great privilege to bring these pagans to kneel before Christ as their king.

Corman was chosen for his learning and his abilities. He was a hard man going to do hard work among a warrior people, as were the men who went with him; they were all specially chosen. No one believed that the proclaiming of the gospel would be easy or that the results would be instant. It was a task for courageous people. No one doubted that Corman was a courageous man. He was used to battling for the faith. Before he left had he talked of how he would bring the Angles to the obedience of Christ; he would conquer their kingdom for Christ. This was fighting talk. But now he had returned having been away for only a few months, and was telling everyone how uncouth the people of Oswald's kingdom were: they were too brutish to learn anything. They were warriors with no understanding of Latin and no interest in the Church or its services. They preferred battle and the sharing of spoils to hearing the word of God. They preferred the mead hall and stories of battles to the Word of God. These people did not want to hear of Christ or to receive the faith.

Aidan and the open door

The monks who had travelled with Corman sought to strengthen his case. They recited a litany of the crimes of the Angles. Were not these warriors priest killers? Had not Oswald's father, Aethelfrith, ordered the death of over a thousand monks at Chester in 616, the very year that Oswald came to Iona in exile? The monks and priests from the monastery of Bangor had been fasting and praying for victory against the pagan invaders. Deciding these prayers were against him, Aethelfrith ordered the men of prayer to be destroyed. Throughout Northumbria, these same warriors had killed whole Christian communities and driven others into exile. Aethelfrith had attacked and defeated Aedan mac Gabhrain of Dalriada, the kingdom that included Iona and stretched from Kintyre to the Hebrides, at Degastan. So near at hand there was proof of desire for conquest and destruction. Even Cadwallon's death and that of his followers at Heavenfield was a matter for deep regret. Had not Cadwallon and his men been trying to defeat a mainly pagan army and protect their Christian heritage? Ida, the very founder of the kingdom of Bernicia, had boasted the name 'Flamebearer' because he had set fire to so many villages. What could you expect from pagan rulers who traced their ancestry back to the pagan god Woden? It was a waste of time.

Aidan was finding all of this hard to listen to. He knew what the monks were saying was true, but here was a great chance for change and for the faith to grow among those who at the moment were pagans. A door of opportunity had been opened; hospitality not hostility had been offered by no less a person than the king. Here was a great opportunity to unite a nation, to bring together the indigenous people and their conquerors in the name of God. Here was an opportunity to bring a warrior people to know the love and the peace of Christ. Hospitality had been offered, an open hand and an open door. As preachers of the word and teachers of the faith they had been welcomed. It would seem that Corman had been too tough on the people who invited him, had shown signs of hostility rather than hospitality. This was surely no way to win hearts for Christ. Undoubtedly strong in the faith, Corman had seemingly met aggression with aggression, and now he was suggesting that it was not worth the trouble of reaching out to these pagans and their stubborn way of living. The heads of the monks bowed in sorrow or in prayer at the words of Corman and his followers. Even the abbot of Iona, Segene, was lost for words. He did not know quite how to respond to Corman. The group of men chosen to spread the word of God had returned with tales of enmity. What could the abbot say? These were the men sent to do the task and they had returned saying it was impossible.

For Aidan it was as if time had stopped and he had entered another dimension. Are we not in danger of attributing the sins of the fathers to their children, he said to himself. Surely as Christians we need to show forgiveness as God has forgiven us. Suddenly he knew that he had to stand up and speak out. A Christian king had sought help from a Christian community; surely they could not turn their backs on him. Here was a king willing to lead his people into a new faith and wanting to set them an example by his own commitment. How could they not take up such an opportunity? It was important that they entered the door that had been opened to them. If they did not seize the chance, it might never be offered again. Oswald himself could hardly beg someone else to come. Aidan had to speak, for the sake of the community and more for the sake of the Gospel.

He stood up and said with a firm voice: 'Brother, it seems to me that you were too hard on these untaught minds. You expected too much too soon. You should have followed the example of the apostles, and begun by giving them the milk of simple teaching, gradually instructing them until they were able to accept more. You cannot force people to be where you want them to be without showing them what they are missing by remaining as they are.' For a moment there was a stunned silence. This was a strong reprimand from a gentle soul. All eyes were on Aidan.

Corman was amazed at the challenge. He felt that he had won the support of many of the monks. It was easy for Aidan to speak from the security of Iona. Perhaps he should go and see for himself how tough it was. It was all very well to speak out if you had not been there. It was easy to offer a challenge from a distance and to make statements about what you had not experienced. If Corman felt like most of us he would have been stung by Aidan's words and replied something like: 'All right, see if you can do better. Why do you not pick a band of fellow workers and see what you can do? I cannot see that your gentle ways and the offering of milk are a way to win over warriors. These are men of war, conquerors. They will not heed quiet talk. They will ask for mead not milk. I fear you will not last long.'

All eyes again turned to look at Aidan. He was known to be a man of prayer and dedication. He was also known for his gentleness and generosity. Could this be the sort of man to send among warriors? Was it not like sending Daniel into the lion's den? Yet Daniel had survived. One thing was sure, this was a challenge Aidan could not miss. He felt as if his whole life had prepared him for this moment.

It did not take long for the abbot to see there was still a chance of meeting Oswald's request. Abbot Segene realized that here was a different sort of person from Corman. Where one had failed another might succeed. At least, in the name of Christ, they must seek to meet Oswald's request. So Segene offered Aidan the opportunity of going as a bishop and evangelist to the kingdom of Northumbria. He asked Aidan to choose a group of men who would work with him in educating and evangelizing the court of Oswald and the people of Northumbria. Aidan felt as if it was all a dream. He had been given a wonderful commission. He had been called to adventure for Christ. Over the next few days he spent much time in prayer, asking that God would give him the strength and wisdom to fulfil his calling.

Aidan respected Corman as a man of God, so he asked himself why his mission had failed. What was it that prevented the Angles accepting him? Too often mission has been a way of conquering people and making them accept our view of life, of seeking to create them in our own image. Too often we have destroyed the richness and spirituality of a culture when it might have enriched us. We need to learn from each other. We need to reach out not as possessors to the un-possessed, for that suggests we are rich and they are poor. We need to go as those who are possessed by God and reveal by that possession the riches that are there for all to enjoy. Before attempting to change anyone we need to walk in their shoes, to share in their experiences. We must also be willing to be changed ourselves.

The blossoming of the Golden Age of Northumbria in a cross-fertilization of Celtic and Anglo-Saxon arts and minds was proof of what was waiting to grow. The meeting of the Celtic culture with that of the invaders was to enrich our land. It was the coming of Aidan to Northumbria that helped to make this possible.

Exercises

1 Look over your life and recall times when you were asked to stand out or speak out for the truth.

It is no use complaining that a meeting failed to achieve anything if we have not set about to try and do something. Look at times when your life was taken in a new direction and explore how it came about. Think upon the words of the Irish politician Edmund Burke: 'The only thing necessary for the triumph of evil is for good men to do nothing.'

2 Read Isaiah 6.1–8.

This is a vision born out of disaster. King Uzziah was the patron of Isaiah. The king took ill. Isaiah prayed for his recovery but the king grew worse and finally died. With the king's death Isaiah lost his security and his friend.

Picture the distraught Isaiah in the throne room of the palace. The throne is empty and Isaiah feels the same. The king is dead, the throne is empty and the future is bleak. Isaiah cannot get the emptiness out of his mind. Suddenly everything changes: 'I saw the Lord sitting upon the throne, high and lofty' (Isaiah 6.1). The Lord God is on the throne, the whole room is filled with his presence. Isaiah is not alone, for God is with him. Sometimes we need emptying out before God can fill our lives. God is concerned for Isaiah and for his world. It is a wonderful vision, but like all visions it asks for action; the voice of the Lord calls saying: 'Whom shall I send, and who will go for us.' Isaiah needs to reply and he does, saying: 'Here am I; send me.' Isaiah too was sent to a people who would listen but not comprehend, who would look but not understand.

Pray: sit or kneel before the Lord and say quietly,

> When hostility and hatred tries to triumph,
> When the hungry cry out for food
> When the rejected long for love,
> *Here am I, Lord, send me*
>
> When the people walk in darkness,
> When your children long for the light,

Where there is a need for the Good News,
Here am I, Lord, send me

Where injustice needs to be challenged
Where forgiveness needs to be brought
Where your people long for freedom
Here am I, Lord, send me

When your word needs to be said
Where your will makes demands
Where your purpose needs fulfilling
Here am I, Lord, send me

3 In Revelation 3.7–8 the angel says to the Church of Philadelphia: 'Look, I have set before you an open door, which no one is able to shut. I know that you have but little power, and that you have kept my word and have not denied my name.' In 1 Corinthians 16.9, St Paul says: 'a wide door has opened to me, and there are many adversaries'. When Paul came to Troas to proclaim the good news he declared: 'a door was opened for me in the Lord' (2 Corinthians 2.12). When he returned to Antioch he told how God had 'opened a door of faith for the Gentiles' (Acts 14.27).

Are we aware of the times when God sets before us an open door? Do we meet opportunities to proclaim the Word and to rejoice in his presence and power? Think of a way you can be a witness to the Good News.

Pray:

God, give us grace
to accept with serenity the things that cannot be changed,
the courage to change the things that should be changed,
and the wisdom to know the difference.

Reinhold Niebuhr (1892–1971)

On firm foundations

Aidan chose men who were skilled at teaching and able to set up a new monastery. They needed practical skills as well as intellectual ones. But above all he chose men of prayer. If they were to win over a kingdom to God, the foundations had to be strong, and there was no foundation to build on but God alone. If they were to talk about God to others they had to know God personally themselves. It was no use knowing the words if they did not have a living relationship with the Master.

During the journey they said the psalms as they travelled. They knew all the 150 psalms by heart and would go through the Psalter each day of their journey. Whenever Aidan came to Psalm 127, the first verse must have made him stop for thought: 'Except the Lord build the house, their labour is but lost that build it.' Aidan wanted to be sure that the work he did was on the firm foundation of being done not just for Oswald but also for the glory of God and in his power. What worried Aidan was how his monks would react to living in a fortress. The intermingling of warriors, state business, war campaigns and the daily services would be hardly conducive to their prayer life or their ability to teach. Many of the soldiers would be far more interested in the sword than in the Word or even in words. Rather than being an example they might appear to be getting in the way, hindering the normal activities of the king and his court.

During the journey Aidan thought of Iona and the fortress of Dunadd in Kintyre. These two complemented each other, they did not try to do the same things. One was a fortress for the defence of the area and for training soldiers, the other was a place of prayer and for the training of men of mission. They needed to be separate if each was to be of help to the other. Then came to mind some words of wisdom he had heard at Iona and which had been offered to men of prayer: 'Live close to a city but not within it.' He realized that if they were to set an example he and his companions would have to also distance themselves a little, so that they could give their attention to their God. Before Aidan ever reached Oswald's fortress he decided that he would have to live outside it. He realized too that this would have great benefits in reaching out to the indigenous people. If he lived in the Angles' camp he could only be seen as part of the enemy of occupation, if he was separated from them he could be seen as a man of God and preacher of the word. Many of the local people were Christians or lapsed Christians who had lost their churches and their priests in the violence of the Angles' invasions. Now the different peoples were seeking to live together. Anglian warriors had married local women. Children were growing up belonging to both peoples. There was a strong desire among many that the indigenous British people and the Angles should become one nation. Christianity could be a force to unite them and bring them into a deeper harmony and peace. Oswald could see this. But Aidan felt if he was to help to achieve this aim, it would have to be from outside the fortress. As much as he looked to Oswald for help, he wanted to show he depended on the power of Christ the king and not on Oswald alone.

Oswald was delighted to welcome the new group of Christian teachers into his stronghold. They were soon made to feel at home. All had been instructed to help the monks whenever possible. In fact, Aidan could hardly believe what was happening after the stories Corman had told on returning to Iona. Still, he was sure that the fortress was not the right place to live, although they would establish a church there. No doubt Oswald was disappointed when Aidan told him his monks could not live in the castle or even in its immediate shadow, but needed distance between them and this symbol of dominance and power. They would have to win hearts through the love of Christ and not the power of the king. Though there would be a church within the fortress, Aidan said he would also build one down in the local village of Bamburgh, as the indigenous people would still find the castle too intimidating.

Aidan was delighted to look out from the fortress and see a group of islands out at sea. Surely, as at Iona, the monks could have an island home. Oswald offered Aidan anywhere in his kingdom. They could have some rich farmland not far from the castle, or a settlement by one of the rivers. The kingdom was large and at their disposal. When Aidan pointed to the little islands offshore and asked, 'How large are those?' Oswald found it hard to understand. Many were little more than rocks, all were said to be occupied by demons. 'Not one of them is large enough or productive enough for you to settle on them.'

'Not one?' asked Aidan in disappointment.

'Well there is one, if you can call it an island.' Oswald turned and looked towards the north. The island that was farthest away seemed to lie low in the sea. 'That island is larger than the rest, though much of it is sand. It has its own water supply. There is good fishing around its shores. But it is not a proper island.'

Those listening to Oswald wondered how an island could not be an island. Seeing their puzzled looks he explained. 'The island is not so far from the mainland as the others and it lies in a shallow sea. In fact, when the tide goes out the sea no longer surrounds it. Twice in every twenty-four hours it becomes part of the mainland, joined by sand and mudflats. Then, twice every day when the tide comes in, it becomes a proper island and you can only get off it by using a boat. As the tide changes each day, you have to understand its rhythms if you are to live there in safety.'

Aidan could see only the advantages in this description. It was near enough to the centre of power, but far enough away to allow them the quiet they needed for prayer. The very idea of a rhythm of being open then cut off appealed to Aidan's idea of what their mission would be like. There must always be a balance between prayer and outward actions, between stillness and activity. Again the words came to his mind: 'Live close to a city but not in it.' Perhaps Corman would have survived soldiers' roughness if he had been living at a distance from them. By being separated from the stronghold they could show another strength, and show too that they relied on God for this strength.

'It sounds as if we have found our new home,' he said to Oswald and the monks. 'It will give us the space and the silence we need, but it is near enough to your fortress for us to keep in close contact.'

Oswald was not sure about this but he thought, 'Perhaps these monks who are used to living on an island would be more at home with the seas surrounding them.' Turning to Aidan he said, 'The island is yours, and whatever you need in the way of help. I will see what I can provide: timber for housing, for your church and the school you will set up, food until you can provide for yourselves. Whatever you need, just ask and I will provide it if I can.' Aidan was learning something of the generosity of the Anglian kings in their giving of gifts, a generosity which was greatly to enrich the Church over the next hundred and fifty years.

On arriving at their new home, there was much to do. Land must be cleared and houses built, or at least shelters to start with. They would need a place of worship that sheltered from the wind, though a standing cross would do for the moment. A farm must be up and running as soon as possible, though at least they would be able to gather food from the sea almost immediately. It was important to get their priorities right, and the list of tasks seemed endless. Oswald was looking forward to the day when a school opened and the monks began to teach the faith to his people. He wanted the monks to be a means of unity between his own people and the indigenous British. Aidan would have to sort out the order of importance of what they were called to do.

'Except the Lord build the house, their labour is but lost that build it.' The words would not leave Aidan. On leaving Iona he had been told by one of the brethren that they would exist for mission, but he knew even mission was secondary. They had to be sure why they were here, and other people had to be able to see it. They were here to worship God and give all glory to him. They must be seen not only as teachers and preachers but also as men of God, lovers of God. Their primary task was to give themselves to God. Mission has often failed because people have sought to talk about God when they have not yet talked enough to him. It must be seen that they enjoy the presence and the love of God. They must show God is real, to be met and to be enjoyed.

Though there were many tasks, 40 days were set aside for prayer and for the dedication and preparation of the site as a 'city of God'. During this time silence was often stronger than words and stillness more powerful than action. An area was marked out that would surround their future homes, the farm, workshop, church, scriptorium, school, dairy and refectory, and the whole area was dedicated to God. A low vallum was created to mark the area out. It was not high enough to keep out invaders: a man or a beast could easily step over it and into the compound. It was there to keep out evil, while all within was dedicated to God. Here was an attempt to build the kingdom of heaven on earth by doing his will. The monks were not just clearing the land but cleansing it from its past, getting rid of anything that would hinder them in their worship. They saw this too as a defence against evil, a protective barrier against destructive demons. Not only church worship but teaching, sawing wood, farming, milking, all of life was dedicated to God and his glory. Here there was no division into sacred and secular, for all belonged to God and was done for his glory. The hands that offered the Eucharist were hands that had offered the tasks of labour. The calving of a cow or the cleaning of a byre were all to be done to the praise of God. From this base they could reach out to teach others, for here they experienced what they would seek to teach.

Once the foundation of prayer had been laid, the monks built their own cells. As soon as they had shelter for themselves, they were ready to take on their first pupils. Each pupil would be assigned a monk teacher from the start. Not all teaching would be done one to one, but each student would need a personal guide, a soul friend. Now the monks were ready to begin the work Oswald called them to do. The first students would come from among his own people, but that would only be the beginning.

All the students would be expected to learn not only words but also of the Word made flesh. There would be classes, but all would also be expected to take part in daily worship. If these men were to be educated, they needed to be educated in the faith as well as in earthly matters. What was the use of filling their minds if their eternal souls were allowed to starve? All students would join in the regular round of daily services. The services would be in Latin, which they would need to learn as a second language. Latin was not only the language of the Church, it was the language of education. The books they used would be in Latin, though these would be few. The speaking of Latin would help to unite the indigenous British and the Anglo-Saxons who were being educated together. At first they would only be able to be present at worship and watch the others, but at least they would be there, acknowledging a presence. They might not know the words but they could bow before God in adoration. And once they had learnt the words, they could take part and then communicate in their own language the wonderful riches of the Word of God.

Exercises

1 Ask yourself if God is truly among your priorities. Are you in danger of talking about God far more than you talk to him? Do you set aside time each day to give glory to God? Have you learnt to praise him in your daily occupation?

An interesting exercise is to break your whole day down into quarters of an hour. See how many quarters you give to work, to sleep, to leisure, to prayer and so on. This often shows if God is given much space or thought at all. God is often treated like an optional leisure pursuit and one that is by no means a priority.

2 Read Matthew 7.24–27.

Sometimes Jesus wanted us to laugh at the ridiculousness of a situation. Here are two builders. The first builds his house on solid foundations: he digs down to the rock. This man is making sure that his house will withstand any storms. When trouble comes and beats against the house, it does not fall because it is built on rock. We all understand this to be sensible and feel it is what we would do. The second man chooses a dried-up river bed to build in and he builds on the sand. We are tempted to say you must be joking: no one would build on sand. But he does. His house will be built much more quickly; it might even be more impressive. You can imagine him laughing at the man who toils at the rocky foundations. Then, summer is over and the storms come. The river rises, the floods break against this house and it collapses. Hardly surprising! Are you such a foolish builder?

The foolish builder did not want to put himself out, wanted to avoid effort. He took the easy way out and went for quick results. The foolish builder was short-sighted. He did not trouble to look ahead and exchanged his future good for the ease and pleasure of the moment. Do you build on the rock that will last? Ask what you base your life upon. Is it physical fitness or beauty, developing your mind or your muscles? Is it making friends or making money? Is it a first class degree or a good time? None of these in themselves is wrong, but they are not in themselves eternal. Where will they be in a hundred years' time?

Are you in danger of trading the eternal for the moment, the kingdom of heaven for a brief time on earth? Seek to discover how you can have a good and rich life now and share in the joy of the kingdom of heaven.

3 Affirm:

> All my hope on God is founded;
> He does still my trust renew.
> Me through change and chance he guideth,
> only good and only true.
> God unknown, he alone
> calls my heart to be his own.
>
> Human pride and earthly glory;
> sword and crown betray his trust;
> what with care and toil he buildeth,
> tow'r and temple, fall to dust.

On firm foundations

But God's pow'r, hour by hour,
is my temple and my tow'r.

God's great goodness aye endureth,
deep his wisdom, passing thought:
splendour, light and life attend him,
beauty springeth out of naught.
Evermore, from his store,
new-born worlds rise and adore.

Robert Bridges (1844–1930), based on a
hymn by Joachim Neander (1650–80)

Open hearts and hands

Openness is the movement from hostility to hospitality and involves a movement away from distrust and fear to acceptance and trust. This is not an easy movement to make; indeed, sometimes it seems impossible. Aidan was fortunate that Oswald was a practising Christian and so made the way open for advance in the preaching of the word. An earthly kingdom is hard to win over for God if its rulers are antagonistic or apathetic towards the faith. If a country is to be won for Christ we need to win its leaders. We need to bring those who influence and govern the minds of others to know Christ and his love. Grassroots religious movements are possible, but it is a difficult task if the political and social climates are opposed to them. We need to win over the leaders.

Aidan was thankful for Oswald's example. He was a king who was seen to be a man of prayer. True, Oswald did not kneel for prayer. He sat like a king, placing his hands on his knees with the palms opened and facing upwards. He could often be found early in the morning, in the church created within the fortress. Amid all his duties he set time aside for prayer. Here was a king waiting upon God and ready to receive from him.

More than this, Oswald was willing to work alongside Aidan and to act as his interpreter. Aidan found the language of the Angles difficult in the early days, but the king stood by him, helping to interpret. Soon many of the people of the fortress were committing themselves to Christ. Perhaps sometimes it was to please their king and to keep in his favour, but God accepted them as they came. The fortress, once hostile to the men of prayer, had become a place of hospitality.

Aidan prayed that the same might become true of the surrounding area and the relationship between the indigenous people and the Angles. Being of a practical nature, he soon had a church built down in the community that lived under the shadow of the fortress. Here he could reach out to the people of the land as well as to those who lived behind the palisade. It would seem that with Oswald's help a door for mission had swung wide open. People were flocking to receive teaching and to come to worship. The church was becoming a uniting influence where the British, who were often lapsed Christians and dispossessed of their lands, could join with the newly baptized Angles in worship.

As these two groups had intermarried over the last hundred years relationships had become easier. Many, though, still looked upon the Angles as the ravagers and destroyers of their people; deep in the hill country Aidan found Christians who accepted him with joy but who found it hard to accept that the Angles were anything but evil. Aidan prayed that the Angles' acceptance of the faith would help to change this as more and more flocked to hear of Christ and to accept the faith.

Aidan's openness towards people was shown in the way he dealt with possessions. He was always open-handed and generous. When he was given gifts or goods he often gave them away to the poor and the needy. As God had freely provided, so Aidan gave. Yet there was no loss to him in this, only great gain. All around, people were talking of the generosity of the monks of the island. Some visitors were amazed at the monks' frugality in relationship to what they gave to others.

Sometimes Aidan bought slaves from the local market. The first time he did this it amazed the locals. Still, like anyone else who could afford it, he had the right to buy slaves and no doubt they would be well looked after. People were even more amazed when he then gave these slaves their freedom, telling each man he was free either to go or to stay on the island and be educated with the others. The freed man was not always sure of where to go and so often decided to stay. People began to talk about this place where members of the royal family, rich people and freed slaves all worked together as equals.

Aidan himself lived as the poorest of brothers, continuing to follow the teaching he had received on Iona: 'Follow alms-giving above all things. Take no food until you are hungry. Sleep not until you are weary. Speak not except you are on business. Every increase which comes to you in lawful meals or clothing, give it for pity to the brethren that want it, or to the poor in like manner.' Over and over he was able to rejoice that he had enough to give away. Surely the true measure of wealth is not how much you can keep to yourself but how much you can give away. Those who have many possessions are too often possessed by them. Aidan remembered the words of Jesus, 'A man's life is not made up of the things he possesses.' He certainly felt rich when he was able to give things away.

Oswald, like all Anglo-Saxon kings, was generous with his court and with his leading warriors. It was expected that a con-quering king would give gifts to those around him, and Aidan was deeply in debt to the gift giving of the king. But, one Easter, Oswald showed a new generosity. Aidan had gone to the palace to celebrate Easter and then to dine with the king. Normally when he went there, he ate frugally and left the feasting hall as soon as possible. He and the brethren would escape the noise and the drinking and go to the church to pray in the stillness. On this occasion, as it was a festival, special food was served up on a silver dish. The meal was on the table and Aidan was asking God's blessing upon it when a nervous-looking servant appeared in the hall. He announced that there were a great number of poor people collecting outside the fortress. The winter had been long and hard and the people were starving.

The supplies of the previous harvest had run out and they were forced to beg. Oswald listened to the words of his servant and then pointed to the silver dish laden with food set in front of him: 'Take this out to them, see that all get something to eat.' There was a slight pause before he continued, 'Then give them the silver dish on which the food is served. See that it is divided among them so that they will be able to purchase food for another day.' The servant came forward and bowed; then, helped by two other servants, he lifted the great dish of food and took it out to feed the poor. Aidan was deeply moved by the king's kindness. He took Oswald's hand in his and said, 'May this generous hand never wither with age.' Aidan later prayed that many in the kingdom would follow the example of the generous king.

Aidan's attitude to food and drink was like his attitude to possessions: there was no need to have more than you really require. He avoided staying in the feasting hall any longer than he felt was necessary. Usually he would retreat to pray. It worried him to see people cramming themselves as full as possible. It was as if some people were like a bottomless pit. This was equally true of the warriors and their drinking. Often they drank themselves into oblivion, and this made Aidan sad, not at the amounts consumed but that it reflected a deep emptiness and dissatisfaction within. Here were people trying to fill a hunger for the eternal with temporal things. He knew this was very much the way of the world. He also knew that we are made for the eternal and nothing less will truly satisfy us for long.

Aidan was deeply moved by the loyalty of some of the king's men. He knew that all of those who were close to Oswald would be willing to lay down their lives for him, not only in battle but in the times between. More than once he had been told the story of how king Edwin had become a Christian. Edwin had married Ethelburga of Kent, who was a Christian, but he hesitated in becoming a Christian himself. Just before the birth of his daughter, a messenger called Eumer came from the south, seeking audience with the king. He was allowed into the court and proceeded to produce a message from his tunic. But it was not a message on parchment – it was a poisoned dagger. His mission was death to the king, for he was an assassin. His movement was swift and skilful and no one had time to draw a sword. Seeing the movement, the king's counsellor and friend Lilla threw himself in front of the blade without thought for his own life, and died immediately from the blow. The dagger passed right through his body and still grazed the king. Though the wound was minor the poison set to work and it took some time for Edwin to recover.

During his illness Edwin promised that if he recovered and defeated the West Saxons who had planned his murder he would become a Christian. He finally won his victory and, true to his word, was baptized in York on Easter Day, 12 April 627, in a hastily built timber church dedicated to St Peter the apostle. Soon after his baptism he gave orders that a stone basilica should be built on the site of the little church. After Edwin's death at the battle of Hatfield on 12 October 633, it was left to Oswald to see the building of the church completed.

Sometimes when Aidan heard this story he was told, 'Just think, there would have been no church in York and fewer Christians if Lilla had not laid down his life for the king. We are not afraid to lay down our lives for our king; the highest honour we can have is to die for him.'

Aidan was touched by the heroics of these faithful thanes. In return he would tell them how he too was the servant of a King and willing to die for him. He told them how many of the early disciples had laid down their lives for their King, and how Christ the King asks for the same kind of loyalty and obedience that they gave to their earthly king. Christ's kingdom can only come in and survive if we are willing to give our loyalty and obedience to it. Aidan told them how his monks were known as 'soldiers of Christ'; like any soldiers they had pledged themselves to obedience and loyalty 'even to death'. At a moment's notice they would leave their community for dangerous places and hostile peoples, all for the love of their King. They would continue in their mission and war against evil until the kingdoms of the world became the kingdom of Christ, the kingdom of God.

Oswald's soldiers learnt to respect Aidan and his men. They could see Aidan was a man with a mission and that he would give all, even his life, to achieve it. This religion was no soft option but called for sacrifice and dedication. As Aidan talked of men laying down their lives, he could tell of the Christ who laid down his life that we might live. He told them how, just as their king gave gifts, so does the Christ; for he gives the gift of life eternal.

In a world where life is fragile and death can come suddenly it is important to know that through God we can survive. This did not stop Aidan worrying about the future of the kingdom. Once again the old enemy Penda was on the warpath. His army was on the move and raiding the southern borders of the kingdom. Oswald and his men prepared for battle. It was a sad day for Aidan when he watched the army move southwards.

Over the next few weeks there was no news. Then a message came that Oswald and his men had advanced deep into Penda's kingdom. Penda had been forced to retreat into Wales. Everyone was hopeful for victory, but Aidan was well aware that winning a battle was not winning the war.

An old and wily campaigner, Penda was able to persuade the Welsh that Oswald would march on them as well as on Penda and his army. In this way the old enemy amassed a large and powerful army from Wales and its borders. Oswald was trapped deep in enemy territory, but it was not in the nature of the Anglo-Saxon kings to flee from battle. He had lived heroically and if necessary he would die the same way.

From the start Oswald and his men were outnumbered, and the enemy soon gained the upper hand. Soon the faithful warriors guarding Oswald were falling around him and he knew he was about to be slain. Just before his final moment his thoughts turned to his God, and he prayed for his friends and protector as they fell: 'Lord had mercy on their souls.' On 5 August 642 Oswald, who had kept the fragile peace for nine years, died.

Penda was triumphant. Here was another Christian king defeated. Oswald's head, hands and feet were impaled on spikes and displayed at the fortress of Hen Dinas. The strength of Northumbria was wasted away. The kingdom would split into the sub-kingdoms of Bernicia in the north and Deira in the south, though Penda was defeated by Oswy, the brother of Oswald and king of Bernicia, in 655.

The following year Oswy came with an army and removed Oswald's remains. The relics were brought north, the head was placed in the church at Lindisfarne and his hands in Bamburgh where he had shown much of his generosity. Though the great kingdom of Northumbria was split and its powers were never fully regained, the Church continued to grow. Even Peada, the son of the old enemy Penda, became a Christian. Sadly Aidan did not live to see this great step forward; Peada was baptized by his successor Bishop Finan in 653. But Aidan's influence would go on. Four priests would go to Mercia to instruct and baptize those who had once been enemies. The light that was lit at Lindisfarne was spreading to other hearts and lands. Places once hostile were now hospitable, welcoming people with open hands.

Exercises

1 Read the story of the man who built bigger and better barns (Luke 12.16–21).

If I were that man I would likely have done the same. There is no doubt that he was a capable and good farmer. He increased his harvest yield. He did not live just for the moment, he planned ahead. Why did he run into trouble?

There seem to be two major reasons. The first was that he planned for the future but not for eternity. He was so concerned for the things of the world that he did not see beyond it. His plans were all for this life, which can be wonderful but which is short, and gave no thought to life eternal.

The second reason is like the first. He saw to the growth of his fields but not to his own eternal being. He set his sights on the growth of crops but lost sight of how he could grow in his relationship to God. He may have been rich on earth but he was poor in the eyes of eternity. A certain comedian was asked what a millionaire left behind when he died. His reply was: 'Everything'.

Ponder   Ask yourself: are you filling your life with the wrong things? Are your eyes fixed on the eternal? Do you let the calls and demands of the world crowd out God and things eternal? A daily living relationship with God is of vital importance to us all.

Promise   Promise to be more generous in the way that you give of your time to others and to God. Seek to keep your eyes and heart on that which is eternal.

2 Pray:

> Dearest Lord, teach me to be generous;
> Teach me to serve you as you deserve;
> To give and not to count the cost,
> To fight and not to heed the wounds,
> To toil and not to seek for rest,
> To labour and not to ask for any reward,
> Save that of knowing that I do your will.
> Fill me, I pray, with your light and life,
> That I may show forth your glory.
> Grant that your love may so fill my life
> That we may count nothing too small to do for you,
> Nothing too much to give
> And nothing too hard to bear.
>
> Ignatius Loyola (1491–1556)

Feet on the ground

Aidan had a great talent for meeting and making contact with people. To help in this he preferred to walk wherever he went rather than to ride upon a horse. Horse riding would set him above so many people, and it presented an image of richness and power. Lords and people of power rode horses, the ordinary folk of the land walked. On a horse you looked down on others; Aidan wanted to meet people on the same level. While he walked Aidan prayed or recited the psalms with his travelling companions. Walking made it easier to pray together than when travelling on horseback. Whenever he met someone on the way he asked if they were Christian. If they were, he would say, 'Let us pray together.' If they were not he would ask them, 'Why not?' And this was always done with a feeling of openness, without hostility.

You could well imagine Aidan instructing his students about keeping their feet on the ground. They should not think of themselves as more important or above others, for all are the children of God. Nor should they be so heavenly minded as to be no earthly use. They must have their feet firmly on earth even if their hearts were set on heaven. Life needs to be balanced. That is why the monastic life was not spent only in prayer. We have a spirit that needs to grow, but we also have minds and bodies that need attention. We need to learn to live in this world, as it is the world that God has created for us. We need to learn to work with our hands, to labour in the fields, to share in the tasks of the community. We need to educate our minds and not live in ignorance. We need a life that maintains a good balance. Like the rhythm of the tides, we need a time for busy-ness and a time for stillness.

Yet there was a time when Aidan accepted a horse. It was after the death of Oswald. Aidan was visiting Deira, which was now ruled by Oswald's cousin, Oswin. A truly noble king, handsome in appearance, tall in stature and pleasant in speech, Oswin was known for his generosity and gave to both rich and poor. He won the affection of many through his kindness, and many nobles came to serve him. The centre of Oswin's kingdom was about 150 miles from Lindisfarne and Aidan had walked all the way. The king, perhaps aware that Aidan was getting older, insisted that he accept the offer of a horse. Oswin felt that a bishop of the church should not be walking like a peasant: a man must accept a position of authority if he were to wield any power.

For some reason Aidan accepted the offer. It would be quicker. He would get to Lindisfarne much faster. But even at the start he was aware that he would converse with fewer people on the way. There were indeed advantages to travelling quickly, but speed was not everything. Oswin took Aidan to the stables and provided him with one of his finest horses, truly a horse fit for a king. He wanted Bishop Aidan to have of the best. In the same way, the saddle and trappings were not just ordinary ones but the best that could be provided. The harness, the bridle, the saddle were all of excellent workmanship and of the finest leather: they must have cost a fortune.

Aidan was certainly touched by such a gift: the king was indeed generous. As he left, Aidan was comfortable in the saddle. But he was not comfortable at heart. This would set him above many people. He would pass by peasants and they would get out of the road for him to pass. They would not want to talk to him: he was far above them. He would be a target for robbers and for envy. This was a possession that could take him over. Aidan did not feel comfortable. But a solution soon presented itself.

On the road in front of him was a poor beggar, asking for a small gift. Aidan could have sped past, for there were many such beggars on the road, but he stopped and dismounted. The beggar was amazed that he was even noticed, so many had passed him by. Aidan had little to give him, for as usual he was travelling lightly. He explained to the man that he had little, but he could have what he did own: he could have the horse on which he rode. The beggar could not believe it. Fear came into his eyes. What sort of man was this? Was it some sort of trick? Where was the catch? Aidan saw the fear and tried to calm him. 'This horse has been a free gift to me. I freely give it to you. The horse and its trappings cost me nothing, so I freely offer them to you.'

The man had never owned a horse. He hardly knew how to deal with it. But Aidan encouraged him and showed how to lead it. He told him that he would get a good price for it at the market and even more for its trappings. Each looked at the other, both with tears in their eyes as they walked off in opposite directions. The beggar's heart was full of a new hope, while Aidan's felt free and full of joy. His journey would now take longer but he would once again meet people on the same level. He would have time to talk to them and walk with them. His only concern was what would he say to Oswin the next time they met.

It was not long before Aidan was back at Oswin's palace. He could see by the king's looks that he already knew what had happened. In fact the whole court had been shocked to hear of what Aidan had done. The king knew that if he gave a gift a man could then do what he liked with it, but it disturbed him that Aidan had so quickly dispensed with the help that he had offered. As the time approached for them to dine Oswin said, 'Bishop Aidan, what did you mean by giving away the gift that I gave you? That horse was for your benefit. It was fit for a king or a bishop, not a beggar. I could have found you an old nag if you wanted to give it away to the first beggar that you met.'

Aidan's reply stunned the king to silence. 'What do you think, O king? Is the child of a mare of greater importance than one of the sons of God in your eyes?' By the stillness that followed Aidan was troubled that he may have offended such a generous king. They then went into the hall. Oswin did not sit down as usual but stood by the fire. He seemed lost in thought; there was something troubling him. Suddenly he came forward and knelt before Aidan, asking forgiveness: 'Never again will I question how much of yourself or your possessions you are giving to the "sons of God".' Aidan at once persuaded the king to rise. This was not a good position for the king to be seen in with his thanes present. They might see it as a sign of weakness. Aidan suggested that Oswin resume his place at the table. The king did so and the atmosphere relaxed.

Aidan, however, felt a chill in his heart. Here was a noble king indeed, but he was not long for this world. Tears began to flow from his eyes as the sadness of this thought filled his mind. A priest who was accompanying him noticed the tears and asked him in the tongue of the Scots, so that no one else would understand his words, 'Tell me, Father, what is it that troubles you?' Aidan spoke quietly for only the priest to hear: 'I have never met such a humble king as Oswin. But I feel he has not long to live. I am sure he will die soon.'

For all that Aidan sought peace, there was trouble in Northumbria. Oswy believed that, in the battles against the old enemy Penda, Bernicia and Deira should be united, and to this end he decided that he should rule both kingdoms. He mustered his army and marched south, bringing his troops to Wilfar's Dun near Catterick. Knowing that the stronger Bernician army would triumph, Oswin disbanded his troops. There was no sense in allowing his people to be killed when they could not hope to stand against Oswy. He then went into hiding, along with a nobleman called Tondhere, staying with a close and trusted friend called Hunwald. But Hunwald betrayed Oswin to Oswy by sending a message to say where he was. From Oswy's camp the reeve Aethelwin was sent to assassinate both Tondhere and Oswin. It was at a place called Gilling on 20 August 651 that Oswin and his nobleman friend died. This action only alienated the two kingdoms and did nothing to help Oswy in his desire for more power.

Sadly for Aidan, his vision of the death of Oswin had come true. His heart was truly heavy, for a gracious and kind ruler had been murdered. The kingdom of Northumbria was being weakened by internal strife. Christians had set out to fight Christians. It was as if the old warrior ways of the Angles and Saxons were seeking to triumph. So much that Aidan had achieved was in danger of being swept away. War within Northumbria could only weaken the kingdom. At Bamburgh Oswy's queen was as horrified as Aidan, and swore that Oswy would have to make reparation for such an act.

Aidan was truly pained in the days that followed. Oswin had been such a gracious and generous ruler. His kingdom had attracted all sorts of scholars and noblemen. Deira had become a good place to live. Talent was thriving, the church communities were growing. Now war or internal strife was threatening all. The Evil One was seeking to triumph and the powers of darkness were being unleashed.

Aidan signed himself with the sign of the cross and gave thanks for the victory of Christ, as a wave of pain swept though his body. He felt as if his heart would burst for the love of these Northumbrians and for the sadness that was overwhelming him. Here he was approaching Bamburgh where it all began for him. For the last 16 years he had worshipped God and brought others to him in this beautiful land. How much had happened, what wonderful things God had brought to pass! Throughout the whole of the kingdom there were centres of worship and places of learning. All down the coast, at every river mouth there was a Christian settlement and often a monastery. Churches and wayside crosses were springing up throughout the land. Education and art were growing alongside the increase of the faithful. Even the pagan Penda, that old warrior and enemy, had said he would allow Christians to come and teach in Mercia. God had greatly blessed this land, using Bamburgh and Lindisfarne to achieve much of it. Perhaps it was because of this the powers of evil were trying to stop any more progress. The thought caused a great pain to shoot through Aidan's chest. The encounter he would have with Oswy troubled him, though it was necessary for the good of the land and for the soul of the king.

Aidan thanked God for Columba and the saints of Iona. He gave special thanks for those who accompanied him to Lindisfarne. He remembered the hospitality of kings, giving thanks especially for Oswald, whose generous hand was enshrined in Bamburgh. He thought of the day with Oswin when the king had knelt before him and asked forgiveness.

Especially he remembered when he had persuaded Princess Hilda to stay in England and to become a nun within the kingdom. Born in 614 of the royal household of Northumbria, at the age of 12 Hilda had been baptized alongside King Edwin by Paulinus in York. When she was 33, Aidan persuaded her to help establish a monastery in England rather than go to Chelles in France. Hilda was given a hide of land on the north side of the river Wear, but she had been there only a year when he made her abbess of the monastery of Hartlepool in place of Heiu, the first woman in Northumbria to take the vows and habit of a nun and herself consecrated by Aidan. He was aware of so many monasteries that had been founded and of the good work they were doing. So many exciting things had happened, but there was still so much to achieve. And evil was always ready to invade hearts and the land.

Aidan had come down the hillside and was approaching the wooden church in the settlement of Bamburgh. The fortress loomed ahead of him on the great outcrop of rock. The light was beginning to fade, but another darkness was coming upon Aidan. He could hardly breathe. His heart ached and every step caused pain as he struggled towards the church. On the rise as he came to the church he looked across to Lindisfarne, set in a calm sea. The sun was setting to the left of it. So much had been done. There was a roaring in his ears like mighty waves, and waves of darkness were seeking to overtake him. Aidan reached the west wall of the church but did not have the strength to enter it. A young monk came to his aid and suggested he be still. Aidan had always found stillness in the presence no trouble, and as the first stars came into the sky he quietly recited the Psalms. He could just see Lindisfarne and he knew it was for the last time; he was leaving the kingdom of Bernicia for the fullness of the kingdom of God. The King he had served all his life was waiting to welcome him into his kingdom. Aidan had his feet firmly planted on the ground, yet his heart belonged to God and the kingdom of heaven. On the evening of 31 August 651 he entered into the fullness of life eternal.

How many lives Aidan had touched and influenced in his lifetime it would be impossible to say. He influenced kings and kingdoms, he taught future teachers and missionaries. His life touched the lives of Chad and Cedd, Hilda and Ebba. Countless unnamed people were brought to the faith and a whole land was changed. Bede tells us that on the night Aidan died, Cuthbert had a vision of a holy soul being taken by angels into heaven. So Aidan influenced even this young man, though Cuthbert was over forty miles away in the hills looking after sheep.

Aidan was buried in the monks' cemetery on Lindisfarne. Later his bones were translated into the church on the island. When abbot Colman left Lindisfarne after the Synod of Whitby in 664, he took some of Aidan's bones with him – first to Iona and then in 667 to Inishbofin, an island off the west coast of Galway in Ireland.

The rest of Aidan's bones remained on Lindisfarne until the second Viking invasion of 875. Then his relics, along with the body of Cuthbert and the head of Oswald, were removed from the island by members of the community seeking a safe home for them. After many wanderings the monks, who became known as 'Cuthbert's folk', were able in more peaceful times to settle at the old Roman fort at Chester-le-Street in County Durham. After wandering for seven years the remains of Aidan, Oswald and Cuthbert were allowed to rest.

In 995 there was yet another Viking uprising and once more Cuthbert's folk were on the move. They stayed at Ripon for four months, planning to return to Chester-le-Street, but circumstances forced them to go to Dunholm, better known to us as Durham. And here at last Aidan, Oswald and Cuthbert would find rest. Aidan is especially remembered on 31 August, the day he died at Bamburgh.

Joseph Barber Lightfoot, Bishop of Durham in the times of Queen Victoria, said of Aidan and his lasting influence: 'Augustine was the apostle of Kent, but Aidan was the apostle of England.' But by far the best epitaph is from Bede, who admired Aidan greatly:

> His life is in marked contrast to the apathy of our own times, for all who walked with him, whether monks or lay-folk, were required to meditate, that is either to read the Scriptures or to learn the Psalms. This was their daily occupation wherever they went . . . He cultivated peace and love, purity and humility; he was above anger and greed, and despised pride and conceit; he set himself up to keep as well as to teach the laws of God, and was diligent in study and in prayer. He used his

priestly power to check the proud and powerful; he tenderly comforted the sick; he relieved the poor. To sum up in brief what I have learned from those who knew him, he took pains never to neglect anything he had learned from the writings of the evangelists, apostles and prophets, and he set to carry them out with all his power.

(Bede, *A History of the English Church and People*,
pp. 148, 169)

Exercises

1 Sit quietly and give thanks to God for all that he has given to you and for the gift of eternal life. Give thanks for those who have been your benefactors, those who have been responsible for your well-being, your education, your growth in the faith.

You might like to give praise to God in the words of Psalm 103.1–8:

> Bless the Lord, O my soul,
> and all that is within me, bless his holy name.
> Bless the Lord, O my soul,
> and do not forget all his benefits –
> who forgives all your iniquity,
> who heals all your diseases,
> who redeems your life from the Pit,
> who crowns you with steadfast love and mercy,
> who satisfies you with good as long as you live
> so that your youth is renewed like an eagle's.
> The Lord works vindication and justice for all who are
>   oppressed.
> He made his way known to Moses, his acts to the people of
>   Israel.
> The Lord is merciful and gracious,
> slow to anger and abounding in steadfast love.

2 Read Matthew 25.31–46.

Pause   Be still from all activity and rest in the love and presence of God. There is no need to do anything to make God come, for he is with you always; relax and make room in your life for God.

Presence   Know that God is with you at this very moment, for he is always with you. Know that God loves you and cares for all that is happening in your life. Rest for a few moments in his loving presence. Allow God to give you his peace.

Picture   Picture Aidan giving his horse away to a beggar. Try to imagine the difference the horse or its value would make in the life of the beggar. Try and see the changes it could make on the poor man's life. Know how much joy it gave to Aidan.

Now picture the poverty of the present world, the starving and the homeless. You may have an area of deprivation near you. Pick out an individual, feel their need, their pain, their sorrow. Visualize their struggle for existence. You may seek information from Tear Fund or Christian Aid. There is always a current problem of suffering in our world. Seek to feel with those who are suffering.

Ponder   Jesus is encountered in the cry of the poor. Jesus is met in the suffering. One of the ways of meeting Christ is through another person. He is there among the 'least'. Know that he calls to you in the poor and the needy. Discover that when you give of yourself to another you are sharing in the love of God, and that God waits to meet you in the other.

Promise   Promise that you will seek to make a difference to at least one person who is in need or suffering at this time. Know that that person is enriching you, for true riches are not measured by what we possess but by what we are able to give away. In giving, you are extending yourself and your love.

3 Pray:

> Lord God,
> who called Aidan to burn like a bright flame in the Dark
>   Ages,
> set our hearts on fire with love for you.
> Let our ears be open to the cries of the poor
> and our hands in the joy of sharing:
> let us walk in the light of your love
> and reveal your brightness and glory in our lives:
> may it be seen that we love you and walk in your presence.
> Through Jesus Christ our Lord who is alive and reigns with
>   you,
> O Father and the Holy Spirit, one God, world without end.
>   Amen.

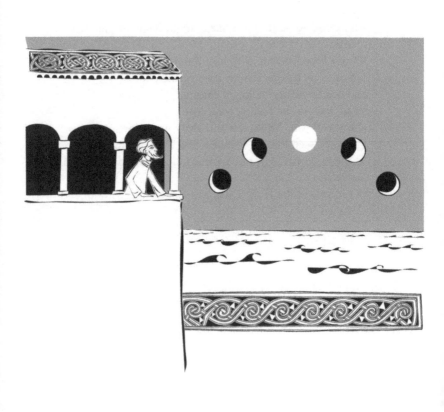

BEDE

Bede at St Peter's, Wearmouth

For someone who writes so much about saints and kings, Bede tells us little about himself. Though he writes about Aidan, Cuthbert, Benedict Biscop and Ceolfrith, he gives us little of his own life. Perhaps he felt it was befitting a monk not to say much about his own acts and deeds. The main source of information about his life comes in a short autobiographical note at the end of his *History of the English Church and People*:

> With God's help, I Bede, the servant of Christ and priest of the monastery of the blessed apostles Peter and Paul at Wearmouth and Jarrow, have assembled these facts about the history of the Church in Britain, and of the Church of the English in particular, so far as I have been able to ascertain them from ancient writings, from the traditions of our forebears, and from my own personal knowledge.
>
> I was born on the lands of this monastery, and on reaching seven years of age I was entrusted by my family first to the most reverend Abbot Benedict and later to Abbot Ceolfrid for my education. I have spent the remainder of my life in this monastery and devoted myself entirely to the study of the Scriptures. And while I have observed the regular discipline and sung the choir offices daily in church, my chief delight has always been in study, teaching, and writing.
>
> I was ordained deacon in my nineteenth year, and priest in my thirtieth, receiving both these orders at the hands of the most reverend Bishop John at the direction of Abbot Ceolfrid. From the time of my receiving the priesthood until my fifty-ninth year, I have worked, both for my own benefit and that of my brethren, to compile short extracts from the works of the

venerable Fathers on Holy Scripture and to comment on their
meaning and interpretation.

(Bede, *A History of the English Church and People*, pp. 336–8)

As Bede finished his *History* in the year 731, it has been calcu-
lated that he was born in 672 or 673. The land on which he
was born was soon to be given by king Ecgfrith to Benedict
Biscop for the founding of a monastery. Benedict had recently returned from his fourth pilgrimage to Rome and was given
70 hides of land by Ecgfrith on the mouth of the river Wear.
(A hide of land was meant to be enough to maintain a household and their dependants and was usually between 60 and 120
acres. This land was therefore a most generous gift that might
have been anything between 4,200 and 8,400 acres; the better
the land the smaller the acreage would be.) In the same period
Wilfrid had restored the cathedral at York and had begun
building churches at Ripon and Hexham. Perhaps Ecgfrith
thought it wise to have within his kingdom a trusty friend
with a power base in the Church. Bede tells us nothing of his
family: whether they were rich or poor we do not know. But it
was wonderful for him that the land of his birth was given to
Benedict Biscop, for this gift would deeply influence the whole
of his life. He was born in the right place at the right time.

Benedict himself was born of a noble Northumbrian family
and was originally known as Biscop Baducing, his family
name. Bede tells us that he took the name 'Benedictus' when
he later entered the monastic life. He served king Oswy of
Northumbria, and for his service as a thane and as a soldier in
Oswy's court he was endowed with an estate worthy of his rank.
This must have happened before he reached the age of twenty-
five in 653, for that was the year he decided for the first time
to go on pilgrimage to Rome. During the next 15 years Benedict
would pay no fewer than five visits to Rome.

It was on his way back from his second visit to Rome that Benedict visited the monastery at Lerins. There he received the tonsure, took monastic vows, lived under the monastic rule and took the name Benedict. He would learn of the disciplined life of the monk for the next two years, and this discipline would stay with him for the rest of his life.

By the time of Benedict's fourth visit, it would appear that he had decided to found a monastery, for on this visit he began to collect a large number of books and commissioned friends to do the same for him. On returning to Northumbria he obviously impressed king Ecgfrith with his stories, his knowledge of the religious life, his collection of books and various relics, and it was at this time that the king gave the 70 hides of land on which he was to build a monastery.

Benedict sought the help of Ceolfrith, another Northumbrian noble who had become a monk. Ceolfrith was born in 642 and began his monastic life at Gilling, one of the monasteries founded by Oswy in expiation for the murder of Oswin of Deira. The first abbot of Gilling was trained in the Celtic tradition, having received his ordination and monastic orders from the Irish, while the second was Ceolfrith's brother. But by the time Ceolfrith arrived at Gilling, his brother had left to go to Ireland for his greater education.

Not long after Ceolfrith's arrival, plague decimated the monastery. Gilling seems to have been totally abandoned. Ceolfrith, his abbot and a few monks went to Ripon, which had been taken from the monks from Melrose, including Eata and Cuthbert, and given to Wilfrid. Ceolfrith was ordained while there and was made priest when he was 27 years old. Not long afterwards, he travelled to Kent and it was likely to have been there that he met Benedict and Archbishop Theodore. He then visited St Botolph's monastery in East Anglia before returning to Ripon.

It is possible that Ceolfrith was attracted by Benedict's collection of books and his interest in founding a monastery. In turn, Benedict was fortunate to gain in Ceolfrith a disciplined monk, a scholar and a priest, a man who could teach as well as celebrate the sacraments. Ceolfrith was also a good singer. And this was the man above all others who would influence the life of Bede.

Bede was only a year old when the monastery at Wearmouth was founded, perhaps with about 12 monks mostly of noble birth. The first buildings were of wattle and daub and would be only temporary; there may even have been buildings on the site the monks could use. It is likely that others, Bede's family among them, farmed some of the land. They would now become part of the monastic estate, providing food for the monastery.

Benedict was determined to build the church '*iuxta Romanorum . . . morem*', in the 'Roman style', that is using stone as the building material. He had seen so many fine churches on the continent that he did not want a timber building, but a grand one in a similar style to those in which he had worshipped. In 674, he set off to Gaul to bring back stonemasons and builders able to use cement.

It was while Benedict was away and Ceolfrith was left in charge that trouble arose. Some of the highborn members of the community refused to submit to the monastic disciplines. (It must be remembered that some were there simply for their education and would not necessarily want to become monks.) Ceolfrith found that he could not deal with the trouble; the pressure became too much for him and he left for Ripon once more. This was a period Ceolfrith would never forget. Even on his deathbed he spoke of a brother from whom he had long been estranged and who, though a brother, 'walks not in the way of truth'. He obviously distrusted this man deeply, saying he would prefer the monastery to be laid waste rather than that he should succeed him as abbot. On returning from Gaul, Benedict went to Ripon and persuaded Ceolfrith to return to Wearmouth with him.

The building of the church now proceeded at good speed. Within a year the walls were up and a roof was on. Mass was being said within the building, though much still needed to be done. Benedict decided he now wanted glassmakers for the glazing of the windows and for the making of various lamps and vessels, but this time he sent messengers to Gaul and did not leave Ceolfrith to face the community on his own. The glassmakers came; they not only completed their task but instructed some of the locals in their art, and this area of Wearside and Tyneside was to remain well known for its glassmakers for centuries to come.

The church at Wearmouth was finally dedicated in 675 or 676 and was known as St Peter's. As Bede lived somewhere on the estate, he may have watched the actual building of the monastery. He may even have attended the church on some festivals. The stone church of St Peter must certainly have stood out among the small wattle and daub dwellings in the area. It was one of the most splendid buildings in the whole country, and would remain as a symbol of the growing power and riches of the Church.

The next thing we know about Bede is that at the age of seven he was given to the monastery of St Peter's, Wearmouth. Sometimes a child was dedicated to God in infancy, for example Elflaed the daughter of king Oswy, who was given into St Hilda's charge at Whitby. We know too that the abbot of Wearmouth at the time of Bede's death had been in the monastery since he was a child, and the nuns of Barking in Essex had a three-year-old in their care. But the Roman educational system declared that an infant (*infans*) became a boy (*puer*) at the age of seven and was then ready for education, and seven seems to have been the earliest age that a child could normally be sent to a monastery for education. In the sixth century the bishop of Arles drew up a rule for nuns, saying they should not normally take girls unless they were at least six or seven; he suggested at this age they should be able to learn their letters and respond to obedience. And Alcuin, writing to the bishop of Hexham, urges him to give attention the teaching of young boys who are in his care.

In the same year that the seven-year-old Bede became part of the monastery of St Peter's, Benedict Biscop returned from Rome again, bringing all sorts of treasures with him. On this, his fifth journey to Rome, Benedict had wisely taken Ceolfrith with him. Ceolfrith wanted to learn more of the duties and ritual that a priest should be able to perform, while Benedict, no doubt remembering the conflict during his earlier absence, left his kinsman Eosterwine in charge of St Peter's. Again Benedict's mission was to acquire books, relics and paintings. He intended that Wearmouth should have the very best in architecture, art and education.

The architectural wonders, the music, the artwork, the ordered day all deeply impressed an intelligent young lad. Bede recounts in the *Lives of the Abbots* the benefits of these spiritual treasures. As you would expect from a scholar, he first mentions 'a great mass of books of every sort'. Very few people would have seen such a collection of books as the young Bede would see and even fewer would be able to read them.

Next there was a generous supply of relics of the apostles and Christian martyrs, which Bede describes as a boon to many churches in the land. Relics would often be built into the altar of the church, as it was believed that this increased the holiness of the sanctuary.

The third benefit was another of Bede's great loves, the order of chanting and singing the psalms and conducting the liturgy as was used in Rome. At Benedict's request, Pope Agatho had offered the services of John, the arch-cantor of St Peter's in Rome and abbot of the monastery of St Martin. Abbot John's other task was to report back to Rome on the condition of the church in England and whether it was free from the contamination of heretics. John taught the monks at first hand how things were done and he also committed much of his instruction to writing. Bede obviously took to singing easily and soon became a very able singer. The visit of arch-cantor John would be the beginning of Bede's love for music, verse and hymns, and in each of these he would become proficient.

The fourth benefit that Bede mentions is a letter of privilege from Pope Agatho, which sought with Ecgfrith's approval the guarantee of safety and independence of the monastery by a grant of perpetual exemption from external interference. This meant many things: it would mean that the monastery should be free from any taxes and its monks free from being called up into the army. It also meant that the monastery would have the right to appoint its own abbot.

The final benefit was in the form of holy icons and paintings, which Bede must often have looked at within the church. He is able to tell us the position of each of the paintings. Looking eastwards towards the central arch, there was a painting of the Blessed Virgin Mary and one of each of the twelve apostles, fixed on an entablature stretching from wall to wall. It sounds as if this was some sort of rood screen that stretched across the chancel arch. The south wall was decorated with pictures that showed scenes from the Gospels. The north wall had scenes from the Apocalypse and the Last Judgement. Wherever Bede looked there were biblical illustrations, added to which were the wonderful colours of light that could be seen through the stained glass windows. This all must have reminded the young boy of the communion of saints and the life of our Lord. Though no doubt impressed at first sight, he would be able to detail all these in later life because they were all still present in Wearmouth. Bede's concise listing of what Benedict brought back reveals the doctrinal, educational, musical, artistic and legal importance of all that was being done. It would have far-reaching effects on the Church.

Even from the early age of seven what captured Bede was the regular services in St Peter's. Once he entered the monastery, the bell would regulate his life. No matter what he was doing, when the bell rang for a service he was expected to stop and go to church. Lessons, writing, manual labour would cease at the ringing of the bell, as would all other activity. And the bell would ring often. It would ring for Nocturns during the night and all would have to rise from sleep. It would ring seven times during the day for Lauds, Prime, Terce, Sext, Nones and Vespers, and finally for Compline. No day was without all of these services, and to them would be added the celebration of the Mass. All the services were in Latin and, under the new system taught by John the arch-cantor, the Psalms, which made up a good part of each service, would be said or sung antiphonally, that is the monks on one side of the church would say or sing one verse and those on the other side the next. The new music became known as Gregorian chant and was also known as plainsong.

At this stage no music was written down; it all had to be learnt by heart, as did the words of the Psalms. Isidore of Spain (560–636) said in his *Etymologies* concerning music: 'Unless the sounds remain in a man's memory they perish because they cannot be written down.' As Latin was a foreign language to many of the monks, they often learnt the 'word' but did not know the meaning. The ideal of education was to help them to discover the meaning of the words and to understand fully what they were reading or hearing. To take a full and meaningful part in the services, it was necessary to learn Latin grammar and music as well as all of the Psalms. Yet the most important thing was that they were there to bow before and worship God. As they mastered tunes and words, how often the little alto voices of the young boys, such as Bede, must have added a new element to the singing.

John the arch-cantor taught not only how to sing but how to read in church. He also gave a good grounding in saints' days and festivals and to this effect he left behind him a book detailing such days when he departed from Wearmouth. This book was still in existence forty years later when Bede wrote the *Lives of the Abbots*. John's teaching was so important for the church that Bede gives it mention in his *History* as well as in *Lives of the Abbots*. And his teaching was not restricted to the monks of Wearmouth and Jarrow; men who were proficient singers came from nearly all the monasteries of the province to hear and be taught by him. John also received invitations from further afield to come and teach.

Apart from proving to be a good singer Bede was quick to learn his letters. Indeed, perhaps it was because he was such a bright young lad that he had been allowed to enter the monastery. As a young monk or novice he would not fare badly. The organization of the community helped to guarantee basic securities, including where the next meal came from. Its members might hold all things in common and call nothing their own, but they were not likely to starve. The normal daily provisions included about a quarter of a kilo of bread, two plates of vegetables, and perhaps some milk or fish or cheese. Meat was rarely available, though it was allowed the young men every now and again. As the monastery was by the river Wear and the sea, there were fishing boats to provide a regular supply of fish and shellfish.

Though the services took up a substantial part of every day, the young men were expected to spend at least two hours in study and seven hours in manual work. It does seem that the work did not occupy them all the time and that they had a good deal of leisure. The balanced day of prayer, study and manual work was obviously conducive to the young Bede. The security and the riches of the monastery in its books, music, art and architecture all helped to make the young lad more deeply aware of the joy of serving God.

Exercises

1 Read Psalm 91 (or any other psalm of your choice).

Seek to let the reading be on your lips, in your mind, and in your heart.

First, remind yourself quietly you are in God's presence. Read the psalm out loud so that each word resonates in your mouth and in your hearing. At this stage do not worry about meaning or content.

Then think about each sentence as you read it again. Let the images and ideas enter your mind. Use visual images as much as possible. Let the psalm influence your senses.

Now let what you have read touch your heart. Discover through the words God's love for you and express your love for God. Seek to affirm the Presence with your lips, your mind and your heart.

2 The monks understood that the words of the Bible are not fully understood just by hearing them or by study. The words

must be allowed to touch our hearts and lead us to a deep relationship with God. The Scriptures are not just to tell us about God but also to lead us to him: not only to know about God but to know him. A method the monks often used is known as *Lectio Divina*, which means 'godly' or 'spiritual reading'. This is reading not only about God but in his presence. The Latin names of each stage would be familiar to Bede.

Lectio (Reading)   Read the passage and let each of the words sound clearly in your ears. Give each word your attention, but do not try to do much else, as this belongs to the next stages.

Meditatio (Meditation)   Gently imagine the scene. Think about the characters. Bring your mind and your senses to work. I sometimes like to see this as trying to make a movie of what is written. Listen to what is being said and see what reactions are called for. Can you see how this passage relates to you or the world around you?

Oratio (Prayer)   Talk to God in response to what you have read and give God time to speak to you. If possible use some of the words as launching pads for prayer.

Contemplatio (Contemplation)   Abide in the love and presence of God. Let your heart rejoice in his love and his power. When your mind wanders, bring it back with a word or two from your reading. Let this be a time of a loving relationship with Father, Son and Holy Spirit.

3 Here is one of Bede's prayers to pray:

> I pray you noble Jesus, that as you have graciously granted me joyfully to imbibe the words of your knowledge, so you will also of your bounty grant me to come at length to yourself, the fount of all wisdom, and to dwell in your presence for ever.

Bede

Or one from the Book of Common Prayer:

Blessed Lord, who has caused all Holy Scriptures to be written for our learning: Grant that we may in such wise hear them, read, mark, learn, and inwardly digest them, that by patience and comfort of thy holy Word, we may embrace and ever hold fast the blessed hope of everlasting life, which you have given us in our Saviour Jesus Christ. Amen.

St Paul's, Jarrow

Bede had been at Wearmouth for only two years when king Ecgfrith made another generous donation of land, this time 40 hides on the edge of the river Tyne at Jarrow. The success and growth of Wearmouth since its foundation eight years earlier had greatly impressed Ecgfrith, as had Benedict's virtue, industry and devotion. Ecgfrith also saw what a good investment his original grant of land had been for the kingdom. It was good for him to have on his side a leading church figure and one of his thanes to balance against the powerful Bishop Wilfrid, who seemed determined to build up the political power of the Church. Benedict was often called on to attend at court and to assist the king in decision-making. The Church played an important part in helping to keep order and discipline within the country.

The land at Jarrow was made up of extensive mudflats where the river Don flowed into the Tyne, the site for the monastery being on a slight rise. The Tyne at this point provided shelter for sea-going ships and so was well positioned for maintaining contact with the rest of the world. To be next to a river mouth in contact with the sea was like living next to a major motorway. The rise and fall of the Tyne with the tide was to capture Bede's imagination, and later he would write in detail about how the moon influenced the tides.

Benedict chose 17 monks from St Peter's to form the nucleus of this new community. Ceolfrith, who had been a help in every way since the foundation of Wearmouth, was chosen as abbot for the new house at Jarrow, while at the same time Benedict appointed Eosterwine to replace him at St Peter's. Eosterwine, like Benedict, had served as a soldier and in the court of the king, before entering the monastic life at the age of 24. He was ordained priest in 679 and now in 682 he was to become an abbot.

The new house at Jarrow would be dedicated to the apostle Paul and was to be built on the understanding that the two houses were to continue as one community: they should be bound together by a single spirit of peace and harmony and united by continuous friendship and good will. Bede says in *Lives of the Abbots*: 'As the body cannot be separated from the head, through which it receives its breath of life and as the head dare not ignore the body or it would die, so neither was anyone to disturb the brotherly love that would unite the two houses just as it had bound together the two chief apostles, Peter and Paul' (Farmer, 1983). Bede is at pains to point out that it was not necessarily strange to have two abbots at St Peter's for a while. It was necessary because Benedict was often away at court and was also planning to go to Rome once again.

Bede went to the newly formed foundation at Jarrow to share in its worship and work from its beginning. It would appear that Ceolfrith was his principal tutor; events and time would seal a friendship that was precious to this young and growing man. For the first year at Jarrow, buildings were being erected and at the end of the year Ceolfrith and his monks moved in. Once they were settled and the saying of the regular services was established, the building of the church began, again using stonemasons and glassworkers.

Bede must have observed the stonemasons and the men who made and mixed cement with deep interest, for he is able to describe in detail how the cement was made. In his later book on Genesis, he comments:

for cement is made from stones which have been burnt and turned into ash. These stones, which were previously strong and firm, each one by itself, are worked on by fire in such a way that they have been softened by the addition of heat and when they have been joined together in a better way, they are themselves able to bind other stones which have been placed in position in a wall. Thus they soon receive again in a better way the strength which for a little while they seem to have lost.

He would have watched the other workmen too; in his commentary on the Song of Songs he mentions the skill of a man who works on a lathe. He would have seen the glaziers making glass and fitting it to the windows of the church. The site of the new monastery was a hive of activity where the most modern building techniques were employed. If the church of St Paul's were built at the same pace as St Peter's, the gable ends would be up within two years. And by 685 the church was ready for its dedication.

Archbishop Theodore and king Ecgfrith, along with another seven bishops, were at York on Easter Day for the consecration of Cuthbert as bishop on 7 April, and the new church at Jarrow was to be dedicated by Theodore in the presence of Ecgfrith just over two weeks later. This must have been a wonderful and memorable occasion for the young Bede. The dedication stone still exists in the church of St Paul, and it reads: 'The dedication of the church of St Paul on the ninth of the calends of May in the fifteenth year of King Egfrith and the fourth year of Ceolfrith, abbot, with God's help the founder of this church.' By the modern calendar the date is 23 April 685.

But less than a month later the king was killed in battle. Against the advice of friends, including St Cuthbert, he set off to do battle against the Picts and was defeated at the battle of Nechtansmere. Quoting from Virgil's *Aeneid*, Bede writes that after Ecgfrith's death the hopes and strength of the English began 'to waver and slip backward ever lower'. Indeed, as a result of this battle the Picts were able to restore their own lands, while around the same time many of the Scots living in Britain and a proportion of the Britons themselves gained their freedom. Bishop Trumwine at Abercorn on the Firth of Forth was one of many who had to flee from the Picts. However, by the time Bede wrote about the defeat of Ecgfrith in his *History* relations with the Picts and Scots had improved, and it is this that inspired him to write so firmly against Ecgfrith's expeditions.

Barely a year after the dedication, disaster came upon the community of the churches of St Peter and St Paul. Benedict Biscop was away in Rome collecting more treasures. From the anonymous *Life of Ceolfrith* we learn of a terrible plague that swept through the country, killing many people and decimating the monasteries. At Jarrow only Ceolfrith himself and one young lad survived out of all the monks in the choir. Other members of this small community would also have survived, but there was no one who could read or who knew the psalms well enough to say them by heart. This put a great strain on the saying and singing of the services throughout the day. The bell would still ring, calling the remaining brethren to worship. But it was worship where only the voices of Ceolfrith and the young boy could be heard for most of the service. The unknown writer tells us of the strain on Ceolfrith and the boy:

> In the monastery over which Ceolfrith presided, all who could read, or preach or recite the antiphons were swept away, except the abbot himself and one little lad nourished and taught by him, who is now priest of the same monastery and both by word of mouth and by writing commends to all who wish to know them the abbot's worthy deeds. And the abbot, sad at heart because of this visitation, ordained that, contrary to their former rite, they should, except at vespers and matins recite their

psalms without antiphons. And when this had been done with many tears and lamentations on his part for the space of a week, he could not bear it any longer, but decreed that the psalms with their anthems should be restored to their order according to the regular course; and by means of himself and the aforesaid boy, he carried out with no little labour that which he had decreed, until he could train them himself or procure from elsewhere men able to take part in the divine service.

(*Life of Ceolfrith*, p. 65)

There is no evidence to say that this boy was Bede; if it was, in his customary self-effacing manner he never mentions it. Perhaps it was too painful for him to write of the deaths of so many of his dear friends. But as he was already at St Paul's and was later ordained, it is likely that he was the young lad. Assuming it was Bede, we can be sure that at this early age he was an accomplished singer. There is little doubt that he had learnt all the psalms, by heart rather than by head or mind because he had learnt them through regular worship. All monks who were to recite the daily offices had to have the psalms by heart. When a boy of 14 at Lindisfarne, Bishop Wilfrid was praised for the speed with which he had learnt the entire Psalter. The antiphons presented a more serious problem, for they changed with the seasons and each one was used less often than the psalms.

Abbot Eosterwine died of the plague on 7 March 686 at the age of 36. Bede notes how, though of noble birth and a cousin of Benedict Biscop, he realized that the monastic profession put him on equal footing with his brethren: in a sense his profession brought him down in the world. He certainly exercised his office as abbot with a great humility that Bede admired. Bede tells how Eosterwine sought to keep the monastic rule in every detail, giving us an insight into many everyday details of monastic life. He took a positive delight in the winnowing and threshing, the milking of ewes and cows; he laboured in the bakehouse, garden and kitchen, taking part cheerfully and obediently in every monastic chore. When it was necessary to correct wrong-doers he preferred to admonish them by word rather than any other punishment. If on his way around the monastic estate he saw a brother hard at work he would go and help, putting his hand to the plough, hammering iron into shape or wielding the winnowing-fan. Eosterwine ate with the rest of the brethren and slept in the common dormitory.

In Benedict's absence, the deacon Sigfrith was appointed abbot of St Peter's. Chosen by agreement of the brethren and Ceolfrith, he was a man well grounded in scriptural knowledge and with amazing powers of self-denial. But he was also an ill man and would not have long to live.

Benedict returned from his sixth visit to Rome to find that both his friend king Ecgfrith and his cousin and companion Eosterwine were dead. Though Benedict himself was also ill, the treasures he brought gave joy to a beleaguered monastery. Once again, there was a rich store of valuable gifts for the churches, a large supply of sacred books and no smaller a stock of pictures than on his previous journeys. He brought back paintings of the life of Our Lord for the chapel of the Holy Mother of God that he had built in the main monastery, setting them all the way around its walls. For the church of St Paul he brought a set of paintings, arranged to show how the Old Testament foreshadowed the New. In one set the depiction of Isaac carrying wood on which his father planned to sacrifice him was placed immediately below that of Christ carrying his cross. In the same way the Son of Man lifted up on the cross was compared with Moses lifting up the serpent in the wilderness. Bede must often have looked at these paintings and gained inspiration from them.

Among the other items that Benedict brought back were two silk cloaks of the finest workmanship. He used these cloaks to purchase from the new king, Aldfrith, three hides of land near the mouth of the river Wear on the south bank to add to his monastic land holdings.

For the next twenty years Aldfrith would be the protector and patron of Wearmouth and Jarrow. The illegitimate son of Oswy and an unknown mother, he had received much of his education in Ireland. He was a scholarly king with some contact with Irish centres, including Iona, and it was due to his encouragement that Adomnan, the abbot of Iona, came to Northumbria and met Ceolfrith. During his visit Adomnan presented a copy of his book on 'Holy Places' to king Aldfrith. Bede tells us that through the king's generosity, 'lesser folk' were able to read it. He obviously includes himself in the 'lesser folk', for he describes how the book came to be written and quotes the descriptions of the holy places. Through the book, he describes the sites of our Lord's nativity, passion, resurrection and ascension in an abridged form and suggests that anyone who wants more should read the book. Perhaps this is one of the earliest book reviews!

These were hard years for the whole country; death was everywhere. Sigfrith and Benedict were both ill, and Sigfrith died on 22 August 688. Before Sigfrith's death, Benedict appointed Ceolfrith abbot over both foundations, hoping that they would remain under one ruler and guide. In fact Ceolfrith would be sole abbot from May 668 until he left for Rome in 716. During his illness Benedict talked often about the Rule he had given to the monks. He reminded them that it was not of his own invention but had been gathered from the best of the 17 monasteries that he had visited during his many trips to Rome. He gave orders that the library he had built up should be preserved in a single collection and not dispersed. He was also concerned about the election of an abbot, wanting to ensure that the monks should be free to choose a man of ability and spirituality rather than being persuaded by rank or family influence. Hereditary succession, too, which was common in Irish monasteries and some Germanic ones, should be rejected.

During the long nights Benedict often could not sleep because of his illness and he would ask one of the monks to read to him from the book of Job. Though he could not rise from his bed, he had some of the monks come at every hour of prayer to recite the office. They formed two choirs and sang the psalms antiphonally, so that he could join in with them, as much as he was able. During his final days Benedict had the gospel read to him throughout the nights by a priest and in his final hours he received the sacrament of Communion. On 12 January 689 he died.

Six years after the plague, Bede was made deacon at the age of 19 by bishop John of Hexham, later known as St John of Beverley. Within the church and monastery there were minor orders that could be conferred on one before being made deacon: they were doorkeeper, acolyte, exorcist, cantor and lector. We do not know which of these orders – if any – Bede fulfilled, though in his early days it is likely he would have been an acolyte. Later, with his singing ability, he could easily have fulfilled the role of cantor, and due to his reading ability and knowledge of grammar, he could have been a lector. Canon law laid down that the age of 25 was the normal age for ordination to the diaconate, so it seems that Bede's exceptional musical talent, intelligence and devotion must have been taken into consideration, though there was also a great shortage of ordained men due to the plague. It is quite hard to take in that Eosterwine died when Bede was only 13, and before he was 16 both Sigfrith and Benedict were dead. The monastery not only lost many of its leaders but also its students through the plague years; it lost deacons and priests as did the church throughout the land.

Bede remained a deacon for the next 11 years. Among his teachers he describes Benedict Biscop, Sigfrith and Ceolfrith in their different ways as men of deep learning who had earned his respect and gratitude, along with John the arch-cantor from whom he gained his understanding and love of music at the early age of seven. He also mentions Trumbert, a monk trained in the Irish tradition and from Chad's monastery at Lastingham, as one who taught him the Scriptures and related to him stories of Chad. Trumbert possibly inspired Bede with respect for the saintliness and scholarship of the Celtic Church.

From the day he entered the monastery Bede would need to learn Latin, the language of the Church, and this would involve learning grammar. He would study the Scriptures, learn ecclesiastical computation concerning the fixing of Easter, learn arithmetic. Numeracy was counted of such great importance that Isidore of Spain wrote, 'Take away numeracy in all things and all things perish. Take away computation from the world and everything is wrapped in ignorance.' Numeracy was needed to tell the time, the weeks and months, to fix the solstice, to calculate Lent, Easter and Pentecost. As Easter was based on the lunar, not the solar year it involved a good deal of careful calculation. Once Bede learnt these subjects he then passed on his learning by teaching others, as he explains at the end of his *History*.

The Library built up by Benedict and doubled in size by Ceolfrith was the source of much of Bede's learning. Here the Scriptures would be available, along with commentaries upon them. Bede knew a variety of texts of the Bible, the Old Latin, Jerome's Vulgate and the Greek Septuagint. It is possible that this knowledge was used to help in the production of the three great Bibles commissioned by Ceolfrith. Bede was the first to name Augustine of Hippo, Ambrose, Jerome and Gregory as the four great Fathers of the Church because of their commentaries on the Scriptures. Isidore of Spain's *Etymologies* was available to Bede: this was a kind of encyclopaedia containing elements of grammar, rhetoric, theology, history, mathematics and medicine. At the time of his death Bede was working on Isidore's *De Natura Rerum*, 'On the Nature of Things'.

At least part of Pliny's *Natural History* was in the library, as were Eusebius's *Ecclesiastical History* and Jerome's *De Viris Illustribus*. There were works by Josephus, Gildas, Marcellinus, and Gregory of Tours. For scriptural commentaries there were many works by Augustine, Ambrose, Jerome, Gregory, Origen, Cassiodorus, Hilary and Cyprian. It would appear that Bede also had knowledge of the Rule of St Benedict.

Ceolfrith had seen Bede's potential and encouraged him to make writing his life's work. While others laboured in the fields, Bede laboured at his books; when others were looking after the house, Bede would be looking after his books and the library. He must have spent much time in research and study, in letter writing and in interviews to be able to achieve what he did. His preparation for lessons often became another part of his writing.

But throughout his studies and writings the daily ringing of the bell would govern all that he did. Bede's life was that of a monk and was liturgically enriched. Once ordained, he was first and foremost a priest. All his writings and research were for the glory of God, intended to reveal his will and seek his ordering in creation. Even the primers on grammar and spelling drew their examples from the Scriptures. The Word of God was of greater importance than mere words. Alcuin illustrates Bede's love of worship and his delight in singing: 'It is said our master and your patron, the blessed Bede, said, "I know that the angels visit the canonical hours and the meetings of the brethren. What if they should not find me there among them? Will they not say, where is Bede? Why does he not come to the devotions prescribed for the brethren?"'

It was Bishop John of Hexham who also ordained Bede as priest, as Bede tells us at the end of his *History*. Obviously from this time Bede was collecting material for his *History*, which he finished in 731, as well as fulfilling his priestly duties. In his writings, he often sought to encourage priests to be better shepherds of their flocks and more devout celebrants of the Eucharist. He felt the laity should be more regular in their coming to Communion. The 29 years of his priesthood passed almost totally in the daily round of services, teaching and writing.

Exercises

1 Look over your regular daily activities and see if you have a balanced life. Do you have time for prayer and study as well as work? Do you have time off from your normal routine as holiday? Look to your prayer life and make sure other things do not squeeze it out. Fix a time and a place for your daily prayers. In this place you might like to have an aid to recollection such as an icon, a crucifix or a candle. If possible choose a place where you can have stillness.

The early morning is a good time for your prayers but it is up to you. Many find that the end of the day is a good time for recollection and stillness.

The discipline of a fixed time and place helps us to grow in prayer. When we do not have fixed times and places there is always the danger it will become nowhere and at no time. It is when we discover one holy place that we begin to learn that all is holy. Whenever I enter my holy place I pause before entering, for it is a special place. Then as I enter I affirm: 'The Lord is here: His Spirit is with us,' or I say simply 'You Lord are in this place, your presence fills it.'

Use this latter prayer as an exercise. Affirm:

> You Lord are in this place, your presence fills it
> You Lord are in this place.
> You Lord are.
> You Lord
> You.
> Enjoy addressing God and resting in his presence.

2 Seek to discover that in praying we share with the whole Church of God. Not only do we share with other living Christians but with all who have lived and are now in the fullness of God's presence. Perhaps, like Bede, you can capture the vision of your worship as a sharing with 'angels and archangels and with all the company of heaven'.

Think over these words from the letter to the Hebrews: 'Therefore, since we are surrounded by so great a cloud of witnesses, let us lay aside every weight and the sin that clings so closely, and let us run with perseverance the race that is set before us' (Hebrews 12.1).

3 Pray:

> O God who has brought us near to an innumerable company of angels, and the spirits of just men made perfect; grant us during our earthly pilgrimage to abide in their fellowship, and in our heavenly country to become partakers of their joy; through Jesus Christ our Lord. Amen.
>
> William Bright (1824–1901)

The loss of a friend and mentor

Ceolfrith had been Bede's mentor and friend since Bede first entered the monastery. He had been responsible not only for teaching Bede, but also for encouraging him to teach and to spend time in writing, and they had maintained the choir offices together after the plague. It was Ceolfrith who had put Bede forward for ordination. For well over thirty years Ceolfrith was there for Bede's guidance and support, to keep the sort of order that allowed him to get on with his work. So when, at the age of 74, Ceolfrith decided to go to Rome, it created a crisis for Bede, who was then in his forties. He writes:

> Having completed the third book of the Commentary on Samuel, I thought I would rest awhile and after recovering in that way my delight in study and writing, proceed to take in hand the fourth. But that rest – if sudden anguish of mind can be called rest – has turned out much longer than I had intended, owing to the sudden change in circumstances brought about by the departure of my most reverend abbot, who after long devotion to the care of his monastery, suddenly determined to go to Rome and to breathe his last among the localities sanctified by the bodies of the blessed apostles and martyrs of Christ, thus causing no little consternation to those committed to his charge, the greater because it was unexpected.
>
> (Plummer, 1896, pp. xv–xvi)

This is an amazingly honest description of the anguish Bede suffered on knowing that Ceolfrith was to leave for Rome. He was rendered unable to write due to his inner turmoil and distress, a state of mind obviously rare in the life of one who delighted in study and writing.

87

However, Bede shows little of his own anguish when he describes Ceolfrith's departure in the *Lives of the Abbots*. The day was Thursday, 5 June 716. Ceolfrith had reached a grand old age. Mass had been sung in the church of the Blessed Mother of God where the pictures of the life of Christ hung around the walls, and in the church of St Peter, Wearmouth where the community and many others made their communion. Ceolfrith had kindled the incense and prayed before the altar. He gave the kiss of peace to each in turn, standing on the steps with the thurible in his hand. Then the congregation went out from the church singing litanies, yet above their prayers there were sounds of weeping. Next they entered the chapel of the blessed martyr Lawrence that stood opposite the main church, in front of the monks' dormitory. Here Ceolfrith bade them his final farewell, urging them to preserve mutual love and to correct offenders as enjoined by the Gospel. To any who might have offended, he offered, his goodwill and forgiveness. If there were any who felt he had dealt too harshly with them, he asked to be reconciled and that they should pray for him.

The company now set out for the river Wear, and on its bank Ceolfrith again gave them all the kiss of peace while the tears flowed. There at the riverside, the whole company fell to their knees while Ceolfrith and his companions boarded a boat, led by the deacons of the church who carried a gold cross and lighted candles. After the river crossing Ceolfrith knelt and venerated the cross. From the other shore the group watched as he mounted a horse that awaited him and with his companions rode off, leaving behind in his joint monastery around 600 brethren.

Ceolfrith rode off with about 80 companions; as he left around 600 monks, it shows how much the monastery had grown under his care and supervision since the days of the plague. And not only had the monastery grown dramatically but the library had doubled in size, endowments had been increased, the papal privileges of protection had been renewed, and many more treasures and relics had been added to the churches. Ceolfrith had increased the amount of land it held by trading with king Aldfrith. The king, who was well learned in the Scriptures, was given a beautifully worked book by the Cosmographers (men such as Pliny and Isidore of Spain) in exchange for eight hides of land: the land was added to St Paul's Jarrow, and was later traded with a fair balance of money for 20 hides of land nearer the monastery.

Ceolfrith also commissioned from the scriptorium of St Peter and St Paul three Pandects, that is, three complete Bibles in single volumes. One Bible was for Wearmouth, one for Jarrow, and the third was now to be presented to the Pope. Single Bibles were rare, for practical reasons of size and cost. Sadly the Wearmouth and Jarrow Bibles have not survived, though odd pages are in existence, but the Bible destined for Rome has survived. Now in Florence, it contains 2,060 pages of stout vellum and weighs over 75 pounds. Each double page when opened measures 27.5 by 20.5 inches.

It would take two men to carry such a Bible when it was encased in a box for protection. It is thought that it took at least nine scribes to work on just one of these Bibles. Moreover it would require the hides of more than 1,030 calves to supply the vellum for this one Bible, which means it would take over three thousand good quality calves' skins to produce the three Bibles. This in its turn helps to show both the wealth of the monastery and its ability to produce good scribes.

After Ceolfrith's departure, the brethren returned to St Peter's and continued in prayer with tears still in their eyes. When it came time for Terce, the bell rang as usual and all recited their office. Then, as they were all assembled, they decided to pray, fast and petition God for a new abbot. A group of monks from

St Paul's who were present and a delegation from St Peter's told the brethren of St Paul's about his decision. Both monasteries were in agreement that they needed a single abbot. Three days later, at Pentecost, the monks of St Peter's and a number of the senior monks from St Paul's held a meeting and Hwaetberht was unanimously elected as abbot. Like Bede, Hwaetberht had been in this same monastery from his earliest childhood. As soon as he was elected he set off with great haste, accompanied by a small group of monks, to tell Ceolfrith the news. Ceolfrith was awaiting a ship to cross the sea, and his reply was 'Thanks be to God'. Once Hwaetberht was back at St Peter's, a messenger was sent to Bishop Acca of Hexham to inform him and as was customary, Acca confirmed Hwaetberht in his office.

Sadly Ceolfrith's passage across the sea was a difficult one. The sea was rough and the journey long, and he became weak. Yet it did not prevent him from saying Mass every day, along with each of the daily offices, and reciting the entire Psalter twice each day as they travelled, though it is possible that with a group of about 80 people available, the psalms were said by rota. The saying of the psalms, which they knew by heart, gave strength and rhythm to their journey. But Ceolfrith had hardly completed half his journey when his final illness overtook him. He got as far as Langres in Burgundy, about 40 miles north of Dijon, but he could go no further. There he died and was buried. The group of companions now split up, some continuing the journey to Rome, others deciding to return for home and report the news of his death and burial. Still others decided for the while to stay by the tomb and pray out of love for their leader and friend. Ceolfrith's departure and death caused Bede much pain and sorrow. He had lost his father in God and a dear friend and companion.

Ceolfrith's Bible, due for Rome, disappeared from sight after his death at Langres. In the late nineteenth century it was rediscovered in the monastery of Monte Amiata, from where it derived its present name, Codex Amiatinus. The Bible's design shows the influence of Cassiodorus, whose Codex Grandior was in the library at Wearmouth/Jarrow. The text is from what Bede refers to as the 'new translation of the scriptures', that is the Vulgate of St Jerome, and is in formal Roman uncials.

Bede again turned his attentions to studying, teaching and writing. Though all his surviving works are in Latin, we know he also wrote in the Anglo-Saxon vernacular. He translated the creed and the Lord's Prayer for use of those who could not read Latin. He wrote poetry in the vernacular as well as Latin. His Latin poems, which fill about 100 octavo pages, were often hymns for singing in church. At the time of his death he was working on an English translation of St John's Gospel.

From at least the time when Bede was ordained priest he had been writing and no doubt teaching on more than the Scriptures. His first book on chronology, *De Temporibus*, and his work on the 'the nature of things', *De Natura Rerum*, were begun at this time. These books show Bede researching the work of classical scholars and bringing his own experience to illuminate and extend what he studied.

He also had a deep interest in the natural world, which he saw as God's creation and having an order that could be explored. He felt it was his privilege and joy to seek out some of the mysteries of the world, and once he had made a discovery he liked to share it with his pupils. Watching the rise and fall of the Tyne with the tide, he decided to measure it and compare it to various phases of the moon. He wrote in *De Natura Rerum*: 'Just as the moon regularly rises or sets at an interval of four puncti later each day than it had risen or set on the previous day, so also each tide, whether it be by day or night, by morning or evening, does not fail to rise or fall later each day by almost the same interval of time. A punctus is the fifth part of an hour, for five puncti make one hour' (Blair, 1996, p. 83).

Bede recognized that the tide in its ebb and flow changed in conjunction with the moon. He went on to point out that when the moon was full, or new, the tides were at their deepest, and these tides he called the 'malinae'. Halfway between the new moon and the full, or between the full moon and no moon, the tides were always at their lowest; these tides he called the 'ledones'. Though we no longer know what these words mean, we know Bede is talking of the spring and neap tides which occur twice in each lunar month. Bede observed that not only did the spring tide come in further, its ebb left a greater expanse of shore. He also noticed how the wind affects the tide. As the main mode of travel was by the sea, this information would be of great use to all who were travelling.

Bede described the world in *De Natura Rerum* as a globe, not flat like a shield but as round as a ball, supporting his teaching on the roundness of the earth by the behaviour he observed of the sun and the stars. He knew that there was a great seasonal variation in the times of daylight in different parts of the world. When it was winter in the north, those who lived in the south had longer days. But when summer came to the north it then had the sun earlier in the day and later at night than the south. This variation was due to the intervention of the earth's globe. This also explained why some stars visible in northern climes could not be seen in the south and likewise stars were seen in the south that were never visible in the north.

He taught that the globe had five temperature zones: two of extreme cold (the poles), one of extreme heat (the equator) and two temperate zones. Both temperate zones were habitable but Bede believed that only the northern zone was inhabited. He taught that everything on earth is made up of four elements:

earth, air, fire and water. Of these elements all things are composed and naturally move towards the centre of the earth. The earth itself was the centre of the universe with the sun, moon and stars going around it. The sun gave light to the stars as it did to the moon. Like other people of his time, he saw comets as portents of change and often disaster. He believed that thunder was caused by wind escaping from the clouds, while lightning was due to clouds colliding with each other, 'for the colliding of all matter produces fire': striking two flints together, or a flint on iron, could demonstrate this.

From study and from observation Bede was also interested in how to calculate latitudes by means of a rod or stick. He gave the calculations he found in Pliny, but added his own explanations, confirmed by experiment. In *De Natura Rerum* Bede provided shadow lengths in relation to various latitudes and for each of the temperature zones. Once more, such information was of great importance to those travelling by sea.

Bede himself hardly ever left the monastery, but he made a journey to Lindisfarne when he was working on the *Life of Cuthbert* to consult the brethren there about his account. At Lindisfarne he knew Eadfrith, the creator of the Lindisfarne Gospels. He also knew the priests Badhelm and Cynemund and the sacrist Guthfrith, all of whom supplied him with their own personal experiences of Cuthbert. Bede received a good deal of information from Herefrith, who had been abbot of Lindisfarne but had apparently resigned his office. Herefrith told of Cuthbert at Melrose but especially related to Bede the story of Cuthbert's last illness, giving a full account of his death. Though Herefrith reported the events the story is told in Bede's style. As a 'reward' for his work Bede asked the monks of Lindisfarne to write his name in the Book of Life, their memorial book.

Bede's life by no means ran smoothly. There had been plague to contend with in his youth. When he was 35 and an established writer and teacher, he was accused of heresy. A monk from Hexham called Plegwine had written to inform him that a priest called David had made such an accusation in front of Bishop Wilfrid. It was claimed that in his book *De Temporibus* he challenged the popular view that the world would end with the millennium, 1000 AD, questioning when the last age of the world would be by recalculating the years belonging to each of the ages.

Bede, who was a staunch defender of the faith and who regularly warned his pupils against heresy, was deeply hurt. He was certain that he had not fallen into the trap of heresy and replied to Plegwine asking how could he, a priest and a believer in the gospels, be accused of such a charge. He felt that the charge was malicious and made out of ignorance, even suggesting that it may have arisen out of drunken irresponsibility – that the charge had been made 'at the table at which one is drunk with the cup'. Expressing how grieved he was and also how angry, he asked that the letter should be given to the priest David and that he should read it in the presence of Bishop Wilfrid.

Seventeen years later, Bede was still sensitive about this matter when he produced the longer *De Temporum Ratione* in 725. He reaffirmed what he had said in *De Temporibus*, but added the caveat that only God knows the last age and, quoting Acts: 'it is not for you to know the times or the periods that the Father has set by his own authority' (Acts 1.8).

Bede's teaching was not always easily accepted. Some of the young nobles sent to Jarrow for their education would have rather been elsewhere. A story often told in Northumberland relates how some students tried to make Bede look foolish in his old age. After many years of writing and reading, his eyes had grown dim and he could not see properly. Some who wanted to make a fool of him said, 'Bede, the people are gathered together and wanting to hear from you the word of God. Come and preach to them.' Ever keen to proclaim the Gospel, he went and preached, thinking there was a congregation. But there were none present except those who mocked him. Yet when Bede concluded his preaching with the words, 'May God grant us this, in the Name of the Father and of the Son and of the Holy Spirit,' the youths who had misled him heard the voice of angels responding and saying, 'Amen, very venerable Bede.'

Exercises

1 Read Psalm 46.

Read it out aloud without too much thought to the words. Next, put your mind to it. Look at the verses one by one.

Verses 1–3   These express that God is our refuge in a stormy world. Picture a storm raging around you and God giving you protection. You may like to read the hymn 'Rock of ages'. Seek to know that whatever happens, God is with you and that your real strength comes from God alone.

Verses 4–7   In an ever-changing world we can look to the stability of God. Jerusalem is built on rocky heights and no river can flow into her. But just outside the eastern wall is a natural spring called 'Gihon', which means 'gusher'. It was Hezekiah who built, or restored, the tunnel that fed this water into the Pool of Siloam in the city. Have you made any efforts to keep your link with the love of God that is ever springing up for you to enjoy?

Verses 8–11   You are invited to know the peace and the presence of God. As a king should bring peace and security to his people, so God seeks to bring peace to you and to the world. The peace and the presence are not of our making; we can only learn to accept them and rest in them. Verse 8 invites you to 'Come and behold', that is to use your insight to grasp the meaning. Then you are asked to 'be still', to relax and enjoy the presence and the love of God which is ever flowing towards you. Verse 11 is a chorus of rejoicing, for 'the Lord of hosts is with us.' The God who was the refuge, the fortress of our ancestors is still with us today. Stop and rejoice at this wonderful news.

Put your heart into what you have read. Adore God who is your refuge and strength and a very present help in trouble. Be still and know that God *is*. Give your love to God. Now read the Psalm again, putting your whole self into it. Use the last verse throughout the day as a point of rejoicing. 'The Lord of hosts is with us; the God of Jacob is our refuge.'

2 Pray:

> Come, O Christ my Light, and illumine my darkness.
> Come, my Life, and revive me from death.
> Come, my Physician, and heal my wounds.
> Come, Flame of divine love, and burn up the thorns of my
> sins,
> Kindle my heart with the flame of your love.
> For you alone are my King and my Lord.
>
> St Dimitrii of Rostov (seventeenth century)

Candle of the Church

In 733 Bede left Jarrow to visit his former pupil Egbert, who was bishop of York. Bede was deeply concerned about the state of the Church in England. He felt that it was neglecting the villages and hamlets that lay in dense woodlands or the remote hill country. He was saddened by the greed and the lax attitude of the clergy. Above all he was worried about the false monasteries that had arisen to avoid paying tax or service to the king. Many of these so-called monasteries belonged to family groups and were not true monasteries at all. He was also aware that many of the English would never learn Latin and there was a need for more to be written in their own language. Bede was due to make a second visit to Egbert, but his final illness prevented him making the journey.

A monk named Cuthbert, who was a deacon at the time of Bede's death and who would become abbot of Jarrow 15 years later, tells us of Bede's last days. From just after the middle of Lent in 735 his health deteriorated. His breathing became difficult and he was extremely weak, though not in much pain. In these last days he remained quite cheerful and daily gave lessons to his pupils. In turn they read to him, though often amid tears, while he continued to say the daily offices in his cell and to sing the psalms. He wanted if possible to sing the whole Psalter through, though his breathing was making this difficult. He passed the nights in joyful prayer until slumber overtook him; as soon as he awoke, he continued to meditate on scriptural themes and with outstretched hands gave thanks to God. Being well versed in songs, he described the departure of the soul from the body in the English of his hearers:

Before setting forth on that inevitable journey,
none is wiser than the man who considers –
before his soul depart hence –
what good or evil he has done,
and what judgments his soul
will receive after its passing.

As the feast of the Ascension was approaching Bede turned his thoughts to the Ascension antiphon: 'O King of glory, Lord of might, Who on this day ascended in triumph above all heavens, do not leave us orphaned, but send us the Spirit of truth, the promise of the Father. Alleluia.' When he reached the words 'do not leave us orphaned', he broke into tears and wept greatly. Perhaps this was a reflection on his early life. An hour or so later, when he had recovered from his tears, he began the anthem again and so continued throughout the day.

The effort of teaching was taking its toll on the old man. Yet as ever he kept himself at work; he was still working on Isidore of Spain's *De Rerum Natura*, correcting it as he was going along, for he said 'I cannot have my children learning what is not true and losing their labour on this after I have gone.' Yet more important to Bede was his translation of the Gospel of St John into the English language. This was a work he desired fervently to complete and one that he would work on with his last breath.

On the Tuesday before the feast of the Ascension, Bede's breathing became more difficult and his feet began to swell. It was obvious to all that he was struggling. Even so, he spent the whole day teaching and dictating. He seemed to be quite cheerful though he expressed some anxiety, saying several times: 'Be sure to learn your lessons quickly now; for I do not know how much longer I will be with you, or whether my Maker will take me from you very soon now.' It was clear to the brethren present that he knew his end on earth was very near.

That night Bede spent in prayers of thanksgiving, without sleep. When dawn broke on Wednesday he was keen to immediately get to work on dictating his translation of St John's Gospel. At nine o'clock all but one of those who were present left, called to prayer and to a procession with the relics of the saints as the tradition of the day demanded. The one monk who stayed behind said to him: 'Dear master, there still remains one chapter left to be done of that book you were dictating: is it too much trouble if I question you about it?' Bede looked up with a light in his eyes and replied, 'It is not too hard. Take up your pen and sharpen it and then write quickly.' And so the work progressed, though more slowly than had been hoped because of Bede's difficulty in breathing. Often the old man would slip away into silence.

At three o'clock Bede said to Cuthbert, the deacon who was looking after him: 'I have a few valuables in my chest that I would like to distribute among my fellow priests. There is some pepper, a few napkins and some incense.' The worldly goods of Bede, who so enriched the Church, were truly very small. He asked Cuthbert to run and bring his fellow priests. Cuthbert went in great distress, knowing Bede was aware that his final hours were upon him.

When the priests were present he spoke to each of them personally and offered them the 'treasures' from his chest, seeking to encourage each of them and asking that they would offer masses and prayers on his behalf. Amid tears and great sadness, they all promised that they would do so. Bede then said, 'If it so pleases my Maker, the time has come to release me from this body, and to return to the one who formed me out of nothing. I have lived a long life, and the righteous Judge has well provided for me. The time for my departure is near, and I long to be dissolved and to be with Christ. My soul longs to see Christ in all his beauty.'

There was no fear of death, only an earnest expectation, a joyous looking forward. For Bede death was not the end, but rather the beginning of a great new adventure. He was facing death with the same faith that he had proclaimed as a priest and about which he had often written. He spent his last day on earth in gladness, urging the brethren to rejoice for him and with him. He wanted them to know that he rejoiced in the knowledge that he was going to meet his Maker.

In the evening the young man, Wilberht, who had been writing down what Bede had dictated earlier, cautiously approached him and said, 'Master, there is still one sentence that we have left unfinished.' After a pause, Bede smiled and said, 'Then write it quickly.' The last sentence took a while, yet at last Bede spoke its final word. The boy looked at him and said, 'There, it is all finished.'

Bede looked at the earnest face of the young scribe and answered, 'Good! You have spoken the truth. It is finished.' With these words he seemed to relax. No doubt, as a biblical scholar, he was reminded of the last words of Jesus from the cross (John 19.30). These were words of accomplishment and not of defeat: he had completed the work that he came to do. Perhaps the words of St Paul from 2 Timothy 4.6–7 also came to mind: 'As for me, I am already being poured out as a libation, and the time of my departure has come. I have fought the good fight, I have finished the race, I have kept the faith.'

Then he spoke quietly to Wilberht. 'Hold my head in your hands. I would like to sit up. It would give me much pleasure if I could sit opposite the holy place where I used to pray, so that I may call upon my Father sitting up.' With Wilberht's help, Bede made a great effort and sat on the floor of his cell. There, he sang 'Glory be to the Father and to the Son and to the Holy Spirit', and breathed his last.

Though he did not have the breath to sing it, surely the hymn that Bede wrote for Ascension Day, *Hymnum canamus gloriae*, passed through his mind. The last verses were most fitting for his departure:

> O grant us thitherward to tend,
> And with unwearied hearts ascend
> Towards thy kingdom's throne, where thou,
> As is our faith, art seated now.
>
> Be thou our joy and strong defence,
> Who art our future recompense:
> So shall the light that springs from thee
> Be ours through all eternity.
>
> O risen Christ, ascended Lord,
> All praise to thee let earth accord,
> Who art, while endless ages run,
> With Father and with Spirit One. Amen.

Abbot Cuthbert later described Bede's death using the same imagery as Bede himself: 'Because he always laboured here most devoutly in the praise of God, his soul was borne by angels to the long-desired delights of heaven.'

The saintly Bede looked forward to the 'light of life'. His final words to the brethren may have been a quotation from Ambrose: 'I have not so lived among you as would now make me ashamed; but I am not afraid to die either, for the God we serve is good.' He died on the evening of 25 May 735 after the first Vespers of the Feast of the Ascension.

Soon after his death people were seeking his books. St Boniface wrote to bishop Egbert and to Hwaetberht, the abbot of Wearmouth, for them, saying in his letter to Wearmouth: 'Send us some spark from the candle of the Church which the Holy Spirit has kindled in your land.' In the school at the court of

Charlemagne, Alcuin, who had been a pupil of Egbert at York, used many of Bede's books. Bede is seen as the greatest scholar of his times, and there is no doubt that among the legacies from his era, which include the Sutton Hoo ship-burial treasures, Cuthbert's coffin and cross, and the Lindisfarne Gospels, the greatest is Bede's *History*. This was the first attempt at a true history by a remarkable man who was a monk, a musician, a teacher, a poet and a writer. He was one of the greatest men of his time and one of Northumbria's most noble sons.

Bede was buried in the south porch of the monastery of St Paul's Jarrow, though his bones were later re-interred next to the high altar. They remained undisturbed throughout the Viking invasions and until the second decade of the eleventh century. Alfred Westou, the sacrist of Durham Cathedral at the time, and a keen collector of relics for the cathedral, then removed Bede's remains, which were interred in Cuthbert's tomb.

During the reign of Bishop Hugh Puiset in the late twelfth century, Bede's remains were placed in their own silver shrine. They were now carried around the cathedral on the festivals of Ascension, Trinity Sunday and Pentecost. In 1370 they were interred in the table tomb in the Galilee Chapel at the west end of the cathedral, but, like many of the treasures of Cuthbert, Bede's silver shrine did not survive the ravages of the dissolution in the reign of Henry VIII. And further damage was done to the tomb when Oliver Cromwell's men later kept their horses in the Galilee Chapel.

Impressed by Bede's writings, Dante named him in his *Paradiso*. It was not until 1899 that Pope Leo XIII gave Bede the title of 'Doctor of the Church', the only English man to receive this title. Yet the title by which he is usually known was first used at the Council of Aachen in 836: 'The Venerable', which means 'worthy of honour'.

Having died on 25 May, the Eve of the Ascension, Bede is now commemorated by most churches on that date. The words that now stand above his tomb in Durham Cathedral, taken from his commentary on the Book of Revelation, express the faith and hope that lasted with him to the end: 'Christ is the morning star who when the night of this world is past will bring his saints to the promise of the light of life and everlasting day.'

Exercises

1 Read Matthew 28.16–20.

Pause   Stop all activity and let your body and mind relax. Make yourself comfortable and seek to still any wandering thoughts. If your mind wanders, bring it back with the words 'I am with you always'.

Presence   Know that you are in the presence of God. You do not need to seek him, for he is with you always. Rejoice in the presence and give praise to God.

Picture   Picture the eleven disciples on the mountainside with Jesus. They must have wondered what was going to happen next. They were witnesses to the resurrection: there they were with the risen Lord. Now he was sending them out to baptize and to teach. Eleven of them, and he was talking of going to all nations. He promised they would not be alone. He would soon be hidden from their sight, but he would not have left them. His words would ever be on their hearts and minds: 'Remember, I am with you always.'

Ponder   Have we let these words enter our hearts and minds? Jesus Christ is with us always. Whatever happens to us, wherever we go, Jesus Christ is with us. This is a reality and we need to train our hearts and minds to accept it. To live without this awareness is to live an impoverished life, for it is to be unaware of the riches that are ours.

Promise Promise to rejoice in the presence of the risen and ascended Lord. Make sure that you affirm each day the reality: 'The Lord is here: His Spirit is with us.'

2 Rejoice in the Ascension and pray:

> Blessed are you, Lord most High
> For you have ascended into the heavens
> And opened for us the gate of glory.
> You came down, incarnate among us,
> To lift us up into the kingdom of light:
> You took upon you our humanity
> That we might share in your divinity.
> You have delivered your creation from corruption
> And brought us to the glorious liberty of the children of
>   God:
> You have destroyed the works of darkness
> And made us inheritors of your kingdom in light.
> Blessed are you, risen and ascended Lord, now and forever.
>   Amen.

3 Give thanks for the life of Bede:

> God our Creator, who gave your beloved Bede
> a deep love for your word and for the Word made flesh,
> as we give thanks for his life grant that we may drink deeply
> from the same fount of joy and evermore rejoice in your
>   presence and power. Amen.

CUTHBERT

Cuthbert and the angels

Cuthbert was born about the time when Oswald asked Iona for help in the evangelization of Northumbria, and he was hardly a year old when Aidan arrived at Bamburgh. Nothing is known of his parentage except that his family must have been considerably well off. At about the age of eight he was sent for his education to a woman named Kenswith, who would act as his foster-mother. And at this stage in his life strange things began to happen, though how much Kenswith influenced these events we can only guess at.

At that age Cuthbert excelled at games. Once, after a swim, he was with a group of lads, all stark naked and enjoying some acrobatics. Suddenly a three-year-old child began to weep and wail and would not be comforted. At first Cuthbert ignored the child, but then decided he needed to show it some attention. 'What troubles you?' he asked. 'It is you who trouble me,' wailed the child, and it continued in a strange voice, 'O holy priest and bishop Cuthbert, these sort of games are not becoming of one of such a high calling.' To comfort the child, Cuthbert dressed and left for home. He would store these words in his memory and later take them as a prophecy of his future.

As Cuthbert was only eight, it shows what great progress Aidan and his monks had made since their arrival in Northumbria. The whole land knew of and talked of priests and bishops; even the children were aware of them.

The same year Cuthbert found he could no longer play games because of some disease of his knee which caused great swelling and much pain. The servants carried him outside and sat him against a wall, that he might enjoy the sunshine. He was alone. Suddenly a stranger wearing white robes and riding a most beautiful horse came into view. The man greeted him and asked if he was willing to minister to such a stranger. Cuthbert replied, 'I would most readily rise and offer you service, if it were not for my illness. I am suffering from a swelling of my knee and no doctor seems able to heal me.'

The stranger jumped down from his horse and examined the knee carefully. Then he said, 'Boil some wheat flour in milk and spread this poultice upon the swelling while still hot, and you will be healed.' With these words he mounted his horse and was gone. Cuthbert told Kenswith what had happened. They followed the man's commands and within a few days Cuthbert was healed. They decided this was truly a messenger from God, that one of God's angels had been sent on horseback for Cuthbert's healing.

More and more Cuthbert was learning to pray to the Lord who sent his angels to care for those in need and who delivered the poor out of their troubles. While in his teens he found himself one day on the north bank of the river Tyne, watching monks near the opposite bank trying to raft some felled trees down the river to their monastery. The wind had risen, the tide was pulling on them and they were in great danger of drifting out to sea and being drowned. The monks on their five rafts looked like tiny flocks of birds riding the waves. Those watching with Cuthbert seemed to delight in the trouble that beset the monks, expressing their opinion that it would serve them right if they were all swept out to sea and drowned, 'for they have robbed us of the old ways of worship, and how the new worship is to be conducted nobody knows'. When Cuthbert heard this he was dismayed. He immediately knelt down to pray, bowing his head to the ground. Immediately the violent wind turned around and blew the rafts to a safe landing near the monastery itself. The folk who stood nearby now felt ashamed of their own unbelief and actions. Cuthbert was learning that when he prayed strange 'coincidences' often happened.

Being a young man of means, Cuthbert had a horse, and it is possibly about this time that he went to serve in the army. Returning from a campaign one winter, he crossed the river Wear and came to Chester-le-Street when a storm arose. Spying some dwellings, used by shepherds as summer bothies but now deserted, he turned in. Having unsaddled his horse and fastened it to the wall while he waited for the storm to pass, he prayed to the Lord. As he did so, the horse raised its head and pulled at the thatch, seizing some straw. Immediately there fell out of the thatch a warm loaf and meat carefully wrapped in a linen cloth. Cuthbert thanked God for this surprise gift and ate to his satisfaction. And whenever he prayed, such 'coincidences' continued to happen. The writer of the anonymous *Life of Cuthbert* tells how, 'when dwelling with the army, and having only meagre rations, he yet lived abundantly all the time and was strengthened by divine aid.'

The great turning point in Cuthbert's life came when he was 16. It was the end of August and the dark nights were returning. Cuthbert was in the hill country of what are now the borders of England and Scotland, accompanied by a group of shepherds who were guarding their sheep against attack from wild beasts or robbers. Cuthbert was on watch while his companions slept. During this time he prayed, as was his custom, conversing with God through the long night watches. Suddenly he saw movement in the sky, a stream of light cut into the darkness. He then saw a most wonderful sight. Angels descended and then ascended, taking with them to his heavenly home a soul of exceeding brightness. Cuthbert gave thanks to God for what he had seen.

Meanwhile the vision began to fade. Thinking he might need witnesses to share this event, he woke the shepherds with a loud cry. They jumped, up expecting to be attacked, but instead Cuthbert wanted them to look at the sky and to search for angels. A strange young man this Cuthbert, they thought, a bit uncanny to have around. Yet he encouraged them to give thanks for what he had seen and to praise God.

Perhaps the shepherds would have forgotten all this in time, if they had not heard the news the next day that Aidan the holy man of Lindisfarne had died at Bamburgh. On the very night of Cuthbert's vision, Aidan had entered into the kingdom of heaven. Cuthbert had been in the hills 40 miles from Bamburgh and yet he knew that Aidan of Lindisfarne had died and was taken to heaven.

Their lives had touched each other, and Cuthbert was sure it was for a purpose. He was in no doubt that God was calling him and decided he would offer himself in God's service. He felt that his life was linked with that of Aidan of Lindisfarne, but beyond that he did not see clearly. Time and prayer would reveal all.

Cuthbert did not know where to turn next, though he did know it was time to leave the sheep with their owners and move on. If Aidan had been alive he would have gone to Lindisfarne, but Aidan was dead and in some strange way this was affecting him. He needed time to think and to pray. He was not quite sure of what he had seen, but he knew who was calling him. This was not fate or destiny, it was a personal call from a personal God.

He was certain too that he would have to go to Kenswith and tell her of all that he had seen. She needed to know what he was going to do; if he did not tell her she would be worried about him. But his stay with Kenswith was amazingly brief. She knew that when God calls we must answer immediately, or too soon the vision fades, and she hastened Cuthbert on his way.

Though he knew Lindisfarne contained many holy men by whose example and learning he could be instructed, he preferred to seek the monastery of Melrose, nestled in a bend of the river Tweed, attracted by what he had heard about its prior, Boisil. He rode to Melrose in the company of a servant and with a spear in his hand; it would be a shame if some petty robber stopped him now. When he arrived he dismounted, gave his servant a hug and handed over the horse and the spear. He would enter the monastery empty-handed. Now that the servant was gone he would go into the church and pray.

Meanwhile, the prior Boisil was standing at the monastery gates watching the young man approach. Even then the prior thought, 'Here is someone special,' though he had nothing to tell him so except a deep feeling. As Cuthbert approached, Boisil said, 'Behold the servant of the Lord,' possibly remembering from St John's Gospel the words of Jesus about Nathaniel. Sigfrith, standing nearby, was most surprised at his prior's reaction to Cuthbert's arrival.

Boisil went to meet Cuthbert, welcoming him and asking him the reason for his journey. Soon Cuthbert was brought into the monastery, though he was told he could not be admitted formally until the abbot Eata returned. In the meantime he learnt the routine that was to become his way of life for many years ahead, a rhythm of prayer, study and manual labour.

When Eata returned Boisil told him about Cuthbert, declaring that he was a worthy candidate for the monastic life, and Eata gave permission for Cuthbert to receive the tonsure and join the brethren. He gave praise to God as his head was ceremoniously shaved in the Celtic style, all the hair being removed at the front of his head from ear to ear, allowing the hair to grow long from the crown of his head backwards. As his hair fell away, he prayed that his old life would be left behind and that he would be a 'soldier for Christ'.

Over the weeks ahead Cuthbert approached the Rule of Life with the same joy and zeal as he had played games in his youth. He knew he was taking part in a great adventure, being allowed to share with the heroes of God. He was even stricter on himself than the rule required, more diligent in prayer and reading, in learning the psalms and the offices. He often spent nights in prayer, sometimes two or three nights at a time, sleeping only on the fourth. He threw himself into the manual work with equal enthusiasm and his physical strength was of great use to the monastery. He fasted for long periods but avoided over-long fasts in case they weakened him in the work he had to do. In all things Cuthbert seemed to excel.

Soon Boisil had taken Cuthbert on as his pupil and taught him a deep love for St John's Gospel. He not only studied the Gospel but also had to learn great portions of it by heart. Again, to him this was a great joy and not seen as a task in any way. Both Eata and Boisil knew that Cuthbert would become a leader of others. He was a man with a future.

Exercises

1 Read Genesis 18.1–15.

Pause   Seek to be still and quiet. Make room in your life for God. Relax as you would in the sunshine. By taking time off from activity, we give ourselves a chance to be renewed and refreshed. Make sure that your whole body is free from tension.

Presence   Know that as God came to Abraham at the oaks of Mamre he comes to you. The Lord is with you! Are you aware of this wonderful relationship that is offered you? Affirm the presence by saying, 'You Lord are here with me. You Lord are here. You Lord are. You Lord.' Now seek to give your love to the ever-present God. Know that God loves you, amazing though it is, and give your love to Him. Rest in the presence and enjoy the relationship that God offers you.

Picture   Seek to visualize Abraham sitting at his tent door in the heat of the day. He is still, resting, for this is siesta time. Looking out he sees shapes shimmering in the heat. They seem to be coming towards him. Slowly the shimmering shapes become more solid. Are they three or are they one? Then they appear as three men standing near him. Abraham bows low to the ground and addresses them: 'My Lord, if I find favour with you, do not pass by your servant.' He offers hospitality while Sarah prepares a meal. In many ways all this is quite ordinary, and yet something extraordinary is happening. The future of Abraham and Sarah and of the generations to come is discussed.

Ponder   There is something strange at work – as there is in every encounter. The Lord comes to Abraham in the shape of three men. Abraham addresses them as 'my Lord' and not as 'my Lords'. This encounter has often been seen as an encounter with angels – or with the Trinity. The Rublev Icon from 1425 portrays Abraham with the Trinity. If I were to ask you, 'Were they men, angels or God?' what would you reply? Top marks would go to those who replied 'Yes'. In our world it is not either one or the other; very often all are there together. To choose only one is to narrow our experience and vision. It is only our blindness that prevents us from seeing more clearly. The so-called other world is not separate from us but is part of our world. It would be better if we thought of that part of the world as the world of the Other; then we might become more aware that we already share in it.

Promise   Promise that in each meeting and encounter you will seek to be more open to and aware of the God who comes to you. Hospitality is a great way of encountering the Other who is God. See how Cuthbert encounters an angel in the next chapter.

2 Think upon these words:

> You are the caller
> You are the poor
> You are the stranger at my door.
>
> You are the wanderer
> The unfed
> You are the homeless with no bed.
>
> You are the man
> Driven insane
> You are the child crying in pain.
>
> You are the other
> Who comes to me
> If I open to another you're born in me.
>> (Adam, *The Edge of Glory*, p. 34)

3 Pray this ancient prayer often used at Compline:

> Visit we beseech you, O Lord, this dwelling,
> and drive from it all the snares of the enemy;
> let your holy angels dwell herein to preserve us in peace,
> and may your blessing be upon us evermore,
> through Jesus Christ our Lord, who lives and reigns with you,
> and the Holy Spirit, ever one God, world without end. Amen.

Reaching out

Eata returned from a meeting with king Alchfrith to tell the community of Melrose they had been given land for a new monastery in the south of the kingdom, at a place called Ripon. He declared that he would leave Boisil in control at Melrose and go to Ripon to help in the founding of the new monastery. He would take with him certain of the brethren, among them Cuthbert. But the move caused some apprehension. Although Alchfrith had donated this land, he was no lover of the Celtic wing of the Church. He was very much a friend of Bishop Wilfrid and supported the Roman usages within the Church. Yet here was a chance to build yet another holy place for worship and outreach. It was decided that Cuthbert would be the guest master, looking after visitors on their arrival and seeing to their needs.

Once life at Ripon settled, plenty of students were taken on. Preaching and journeys of mission were accomplished. There was a constant stream of visitors, including many poor people who sought food or shelter. During the winter the numbers of hungry poor increased. Cuthbert as guest master treated each stranger with great care and dignity, as was the custom. Did not Christ say, 'As much as you did it to the least of these, you did it to me'?

The words often came to Cuthbert's mind from the Epistle to the Hebrews: 'Forget not to show your love to strangers, for thereby some have entertained angels unawares.' He thought this was a wonderful text, and considered what strange disguises the angels might wear if this were true. He thought upon the story of St Martin, a soldier for Christ, who while still a catechumen had given his cloak to a beggar, only to discover that night that in the beggar he had met the Christ. Cuthbert felt he needed to take great care in dealing with any individual, for in each one there was a chance of meeting with God.

Early one morning, going from the inner buildings of the monastery to the guests' chamber, he came across a young man. As ever, he set about to care for the stranger and see to his needs. He gave him water to wash his hands; then, as was his custom, he washed the man's feet and wiped them with a towel. The man's feet were icy cold so Cuthbert placed them on his lap and rubbed them with his hands to bring warmth back into them. The young man seemed to be weary from travelling a long way. Cuthbert requested him to stay, as the morning's bread was not ready. At first the youth refused, saying that he must leave because the place to which he was hastening was far distant. After much persuading Cuthbert left the youth while he went to prayers.

Once prayers were over it was time to eat. Cuthbert set a table before the visitor and placed food on it, saying, 'I pray you brother, refresh yourself while I go and bring you a warm loaf, for I expect they are now out of the oven.'

He was not away long but when he returned there was no sign of the guest. He went to the door, but there were no signs of footsteps in the freshly fallen snow. No one could have left the building without leaving prints in the snow. Wondering how the youth could have disappeared, Cuthbert replaced the table in the storehouse. As he entered, he was aware of a wonderfully fragrant smell. Looking around to see where the fragrance was coming from, he saw three warm loaves of unusual whiteness and excellence. He had sought to feed a visitor and here he had received food himself. Cuthbert was sure that he had been visited yet again by an angel.

Life at Ripon did not consist entirely of visions. It was often hard work. The little group were often stretched to their limits by the demands made upon them. Plague was again ravaging the whole of the countryside, and the monks helped in caring for the sick and burying the dead. Some of the brethren had died of the plague, as had some of the students.

There were also upheavals in church and state. Rumour had it that the kingdom itself was not very secure. Bishop Wilfrid returned from the continent in 660 and received a very friendly welcome from Alchfrith. Wilfrid had received the Roman tonsure while on the continent, and Alchfrith gave him lands that had been seized from British Christians in the kingdom of Rheged (an area now mainly in Cumbria) and also the monastery and its lands at Ripon. Abbot Eata, along with Cuthbert and the rest of the brethren, were being driven out and had to head back for Melrose. There were signs that the Celtic wing of the Church was under threat. And there were still other troubles ahead.

When Cuthbert returned to Melrose he wondered why he did not rejoice, for a great weariness had overcome him. Soon it was obvious that he had caught the plague. The 'sickness' was upon him and for a while it seemed that he would die. Fearful that they might lose such a dedicated member of their community, the monks spent the whole night watching and praying for his safety. In the morning one of the brethren told Cuthbert of their vigil of prayers, for they had done this without his knowledge. Immediately he replied, 'And why do I lie here? I do not doubt that God has not despised the prayers of so many good men. Give me my staff and shoes.' He then arose and tried to walk, leaning on his staff. From that moment his strength slowly returned, a little more each day, and gradually he recovered his health, though from that time on he was troubled with inner pains which never left him.

When Boisil saw how Cuthbert had recovered it gladdened his heart, but he was now struggling with the same disease.

Knowing that he did not have long to live, he called Cuthbert to him. Certain that Cuthbert had been saved for a purpose, he wanted to relate this to him. 'See how you have been delivered from this affliction. You will not be stricken by it again, nor will you die now. However, my death is near at hand. I want you to learn from me as long as I am able to teach you. Not more than seven days remain in which I shall have sufficient health of body and strength of tongue to teach you.' Sadly, Cuthbert knew Boisil's words were true. He hid his sorrow by asking, 'What is best for us to read so that we can finish it in a week?' Boisil seemed to gather strength as he replied, 'The evangelist John. I have a book of seven gatherings [vellum pages of St John's gospel gathered together] of which we can go through one gathering each day, with the Lord's help, reading it and discussing it between ourselves so far as it is necessary.'

This is what they did. At Boisil's request, they did not speak in an academic fashion but dealt with matters of faith that works by love. They purposely avoided matters of dispute and used the Gospel of John to centre their minds and hearts on God, employing the time in meditation rather than conversation or analysis. For Cuthbert these were very precious hours. Not only was he privileged to look after his ailing prior and friend, but Boisil also talked to him about his own future, telling him among other things that one day he would be made a bishop. Strange to think that way back when he was only eight a child of three had told him much the same.

The idea did not thrill Cuthbert. He did not want to be involved in the government of church or state. He would rather be a hermit than a bishop; he would have preferred to be told he could live in the desert for the love of God. He answered, 'Even if I could hide myself in a tiny dwelling on a rock, where the waves of the swelling ocean surrounded me on every side, even if I was shut off from the sight and knowledge of men, I would not feel safe. I would still not consider myself to be free from the snares of a deceptive world. Even there, in my own hermitage, I should fear lest the love of wealth should tempt me and somehow snatch me away.' Boisil smiled in sympathy at Cuthbert's words.

The last readings from St John were on the resurrection and eternal life, and they were especially dear to both men. Cuthbert would remember for ever Boisil's last amen as he finished the readings and closed the book. It was the end of their time of reading the Gospel and the end of Boisil's time on earth.

After Boisil's death, Cuthbert became prior of Melrose. Still in his twenties, his life was now filled with teaching and spiritual direction. The monastery received from him wise advice on the keeping of the rule of life. He taught by his own example of love and joy for the life he lived. His other delight was to go out in mission.

Often Cuthbert chose to go out into the deep hill country where few others ventured to travel. There are many caves and shelters in the north-east where he stayed on his travels. Sometimes he went on horseback, but more often he travelled on foot. When he arrived at a settlement his presence was enough to bring the community out to meet him. The people loved to hear stories and Cuthbert was able to preach the Gospel to them. If he came across a community that had a Christian presence he would celebrate the Eucharist. For this he carried a small altar of oak with five crosses carved into it, one at each corner and the fifth in the centre, depicting the wounds of Christ. Often Cuthbert was away from Melrose for almost a month at a time in this mission of preaching and caring for the poor. Many came to him, making their confessions and seeking forgiveness, while others accepted the faith and were baptized. He helped to free people who were bound by superstition and idolatry.

On most journeys Cuthbert took a companion, often some-one whom he was instructing in the ways of outreach and mission. On one such occasion he took a young monk, whom he was teaching by word and by example. They first headed south, then along the river Teviot. As ever they recited the psalms and portions of the Scriptures as they went. Cuthbert would recite the verse of a psalm and expect his companion to say the next verse. If the young man faltered, then Cuthbert would say the verse and get the young man to repeat it. Often they would go back to the beginning of the psalm and say it again. Cuthbert was a true peripatetic teacher, for he taught as he walked.

On Wednesdays and Fridays the journey was harder because they fasted until three in the afternoon, not eating until after the hour that Jesus died on the cross. Sometimes this was made more difficult for them by the hill people's hospitality. Though often poor, these people were always willing to share their food with a traveller, especially a man of God, and in one outlying farmstead they were offered a meal. Cuthbert declined, telling them that they were fasting, and then preached the Gospel to them.

After blessing the family, he and his companion left for the hill country. When they had gone a good distance, Cuthbert asked the young man, 'Where will we find food here today?' The boy was at a loss to reply, feeling that there was no one around who could feed them. Cuthbert told him to cheer up and have faith: 'The Lord will provide for us today, as he always does.' He then pointed to an eagle flying high overhead. 'See that bird flying high above us. It is possible for God to refresh us by the ministrations of the eagle.'

The young man was not sure what Cuthbert was suggesting. But as they travelled further along the river, they saw the eagle settled on the bank with a fish in its claws. Cuthbert said, 'Run and see what food the eagle has brought us from the Lord.' This the young man did, bringing back a large fish that the eagle had just taken from the river. But Cuthbert said, 'What have you done, my son? Why have you not given our handmaiden her share? Cut it quickly in half and take her the share which she deserves for ministering to us.'

Doing this, the young man now thought, 'How wonderful, we truly have rich fare.' But Cuthbert said again, 'There is more food here than we need. Let us now seek out a poor household and we will share the fish with them. We just cannot keep this to ourselves.'

Though the young man was probably a little reluctant, he felt there was something deeper at work here and agreed. They went on until they reached such a household and presented the fish to them. The family cooked the fish gently before sharing it out, and in the same way Cuthbert shared the Gospel with them. There is little wonder that he was so loved by the people of the Northumbrian hill country.

On another occasion Cuthbert was invited to the abbey of Coldingham. Ebba, the sister of Oswald and the present king Oswy, was the abbess there of a monastery that contained both men and women. When she requested Cuthbert to come to Coldingham it felt like a royal command, yet he knew her humility and that she invited him for the benefit of the monastery. The monastery stood high on the cliffs north of Lindisfarne and overlooking the North Sea; from the cliff tops the island could be seen in the far distance to the south and the Firth of Forth to the north. Cuthbert enjoyed watching the gannets like strings of pearls sweeping across the sea on fishing expeditions from the mighty Bass Rock just off the coast. He would listen to the sound of the kittiwakes and watch the guillemots. If he was fortunate he might even glimpse a puffin or two in the summer months.

Great demands were made of Cuthbert and between leading prayers and intensive periods of teaching he would go for short walks to refresh himself. Amid all the activity, though he worshipped with the community, he often sought time for quiet prayer, and on these occasions he would descend the cliffs to be near the sea.

One night, one of the brothers decided to follow him secretly, curious to see what Cuthbert was doing all night. With the spy following him, Cuthbert descended to the sea and entered the water until it came up to his neck. There in the water, with arms outstretched, he spent the night giving praise to God and singing to the sound of the waves. At daybreak, he went on to the shore and began to pray again, kneeling on the sand. While he was doing this, two otters ran out of the sea and rubbed themselves against his legs and feet as if to dry them. Cuthbert blessed the creatures and they returned into the sea. Then he made his way to the monastery church for the singing of the canonical hymns at their appointed hour.

The watching monk was filled with fear. What he had seen was too strange to capture in a few words. He had been privileged to see something special, but he was sure Cuthbert was aware of his spying. He approached Cuthbert, and stretching himself on the ground asked for forgiveness, not doubting Cuthbert knew what he had done. 'What is the matter, brother? What have you done? Have you been spying on me in my nightly vigil?'

The poor man was too fearful to respond. Cuthbert then said, 'Brother, you are forgiven. But on one condition, that you promise to tell no one of this until after my death.' The promise was given and Cuthbert blessed the brother. He kept his promise and told no one until Cuthbert's death; but then he told as many people as he could.

Not long after this Cuthbert travelled even further north. Accompanied by two of his brothers, he went by sea one winter to the land of the Pictish tribe called the Niduari. They arrived shortly after Christmas, but in good weather and expecting to make a speedy return, and for this reason they took no provisions with them. But things did not go according to plan. A great storm arose, the snow hampered their movements and they took shelter.

As the feast of the Epiphany approached Cuthbert spoke gently to his weary companions, 'Why do we stay here as if we were in a safe place? It will not be long before the twin enemies of hunger and cold defeat us. The land is grim with snow and the clouds heavy, the wind and waves are against us. There is no human help near at hand. Let us call upon the Lord to help us. The Lord is with us who opened up a path in the Red Sea for his people and fed them in a wondrous manner. The Lord is with us who fed his people in the wilderness. So he may have mercy upon us in our danger. He will not allow us to remain fasting on this holy day. Do not let us waver in our faith.'

With such words Cuthbert encouraged his weary companions. He led them to the shore, where they found three pieces of dolphin flesh awaiting them. It was as if someone had cut the flesh and prepared it for cooking. How it came there they did not ask, but kneeling down they gave thanks to God. Then Cuthbert said: 'Now, you see what divine favour comes from trusting and hoping in the Lord. He has prepared food for us and showed us how many days we will be here by the amount of pieces he has given us.' As he said, after three days the storm ceased and on the fourth day the sea was calm enough for them to return south. Here was a strange man, and strange things happened when he was present.

We have here a glimpse of the prior of Melrose, often on his travels, preaching and teaching. He visited many villages and hamlets, caring for people and giving them the sacraments. Melrose was a mission station as well as a monastery, a place of outreach as well as prayer. In Cuthbert and his brethren the active life and the contemplative were seen as one, each enriching the other.

Exercises

1 **Pause**   Seek a quiet place. Relax: let the tensions go out of your body, put all troubled thoughts out of your mind . . . Make space in your life for something to happen . . . Make room for God. Breathe deeply and slowly . . . with each breath seek to be at rest and at peace. Be still . . .

Presence   . . . and know that God is with you. Do not try to do anything. Rest in the presence. Let God refresh you and give you his peace. Let the peace of God fill your heart and your mind. Relax in God's presence as you would in the sunshine or with a friend. Enjoy knowing he is with you now and always.

Picture   Visualize the story of Cuthbert and the eagle. See how the eagle provides both Cuthbert and the boy with the fish. They share with the eagle as the eagle has given to them. Now see how they cannot keep this 'good food' to themselves. As they have received, so they must give. Visualize them finding a poor family and providing them with the fish. See how the fish is gently cooked in the pot.

Ponder   Do you see something greater at work? St John's symbol is the eagle: does the eagle represent St John's Gospel? The Gospel provided the young man and Cuthbert with refreshment as they travelled. Cuthbert taught the young man that the Gospel needs us to bring our experience to bear upon it. We cannot just take from the Gospel; we need to give ourselves to it. Once you receive the fish (the Greek word *ichthus*, meaning fish, is the symbol that stands for 'Jesus Christ Son of God, Saviour'), this great gift, you cannot possibly keep it to yourself. Are you ready and willing to share Christ with others? Notice that the fish is not just gobbled, it is gently cooked. We do not just thrust the Gospel at people, but encourage them to meditate upon the Word. Do you see this dialectic at work? It is not 'either . . . or', it is 'both . . . and'. And it is something even greater. If you were asked, 'Was it an eagle or St John that refreshed them?' the answer would be 'Yes'!

Promise Promise to recall the fact of God's presence during the day and allow him to refresh you. You may like to promise that you will share this Good News with someone else. Such wonderful knowledge cannot be kept to ourselves.

2 Pray (or sing):

> Drop thy still dews of quietness
> till all our strivings cease;
> take from our souls the strain and stress,
> and let our ordered lives confess
> the beauty of thy peace,
> the beauty of thy peace.
>
> Breathe through the heats of our desire
> thy coolness and thy balm;
> let sense be dumb, let flesh retire;
> speak through the earthquake, wind and fire,
> O still small voice of calm!
> O still small voice of calm!
>
> John Greenleaf Whittier (1807–92)

Lindisfarne

The Synod of Whitby in 664 had far-reaching results for the Church. The decision that the whole Church should use the Roman rather than the Celtic calculation for Easter obviously expressed a desire for unity. It was also necessary to be in line with most of Europe: already parts of Ireland were using the Roman calculation for Easter. It was not good for one group to be celebrating Easter while some of their neighbours were still in Lent. Unity was necessary within the Church. And another, more noticeable result of the Synod was that the monks of Melrose and Lindisfarne were now allowing their hair to grow at the front, and shaving it on top in the Roman style of tonsure.

Abbot Colman of Lindisfarne, seeing that his teachings had been rejected at the synod, decided to leave for Ireland and to take with him all the Irish and 30 English monks who did not agree with the synod's decisions. Many monks left for Ireland taking with them some of the bones of their founder Aidan. Tuda was made bishop of Lindisfarne in place of Colman. But Tuda's time was to be short. On 3 May 664 there was an eclipse of the sun in the morning, which all saw as a foretelling of evil. Whether they were right or wrong, a plague suddenly swept the country and decimated the population. Bishop Tuda was among the victims, and Eata was moved from Melrose to become abbot of Lindisfarne. Colman had actually asked king Oswy that Eata might follow him as abbot, for Eata had been among the first 12 English boys taught by Aidan. Soon after Tuda's death Eata was consecrated as the bishop of Lindisfarne.

It would seem that Cuthbert lived quietly at Melrose while all these events were taking place, teaching and helping to run the monastery, going out in mission, continuing to preach and to heal. Now he was invited by Eata to go with him to Lindisfarne. The vision that he had seen when he was 16 was now coming to fulfilment. He was appointed as prior of Lindisfarne and called to help to reconcile the differences that still divided the community. The Synod of Whitby had not resolved everything; there were still divisions over the 'Roman' and 'Celtic' practices. Cuthbert knew he had to be a diplomat and avoid becoming angry with the dissenting brethren. He introduced a Rule of Life, taken from the best of the rules he knew, whether Roman or Celtic. Whenever a dispute among the monks about their way of life became overheated, Cuthbert would calmly rise from his chair and leave the room, bringing the chapter meeting to an end. The next day he would return and ask the brethren to sort out their differences as if yesterday's troubles had never happened. If the argument again become overheated, Cuthbert would dissolve the meeting once more, and this would continue until a more peaceful settlement and agreement was found. Yet amid the difficulties and the wrangling, he managed to keep calm and cheerful.

Soon life settled into a more regular routine of teaching the monks and going off to teach or preach elsewhere. The brethren were often overawed by the love and devotion that Cuthbert showed as he celebrated the Mass, and it was noticed that he could not celebrate the holy mysteries without tears in his eyes. Moreover, when sinners made their confessions to him, it was Cuthbert who was often reduced to tears.

Throughout the area Cuthbert became known as a healer and a man of God. He grappled with demons, quenched fires by prayer, and cured many who were sick. Soon people were flocking to see him and to hear him. Wherever he went crowds followed. Many came to the island for advice or merely for contact with him. There was hardly a day that was not busy. Though his day was still controlled by the bell calling him to worship, Cuthbert continued his own night vigils. Sometimes he would seek out a quiet place on the north side of the island. At other times he would choose the little island of Hobthrush, not far from the monastery but cut off from Lindisfarne for about six hours each tide, giving him time to meditate and sing psalms on his own. He never seemed to need much sleep; sometimes he still slept properly only one night out of three or four. His preference was to keep awake as much as possible: he used to say, 'No one ever annoys me by awakening me from sleep. In fact anyone who does this makes me glad, for by awakening me out of the drowsiness of sleep, he is making me do something useful.' Cuthbert often worked with his hands to drive away drowsiness, or he would walk around the island at night, singing his psalms to keep himself alert.

Life continued to be busy throughout the 12 years that Cuthbert was prior, and he began to long for a more solitary life where he could spend his time wrestling against evil and giving his love to God. He wanted to prepare himself for entry into the fullness of God's kingdom, to spend more time before his Lord and Master. In 676 he was given permission from his superiors to go to Greater Farne. This was a proper island, not far from Bamburgh but totally cut off by the sea. He was told the island was inhabited by demons, but this did not deter the soldier of Christ. He built a dwelling of rough stones, consisting of a place of prayer and a place to live in. Another house was built near the landing stage to accommodate any who visited him, with a well nearby for their use.

Now he had time to enjoy the friendship of the birds, though it was not always easy. One day, while he was at work on the small patch of garden that he cultivated, he saw two of the black birds that Bede calls ravens, pulling at the thatch from the guesthouse and taking it away for their nest. He gently asked them to stop spoiling the guest quarters, but they ignored his plea. Stronger measures were clearly necessary; he said, 'In the name of Jesus, I command you to go away.' The birds flew off immediately and made for the mainland.

Three days later one returned, with drooping wing and croaking voice. Convinced it sought forgiveness and wanted to live in harmony, Cuthbert forgave the deed and the bird flew off once more. But soon both birds returned, the second flying slowly as it was carrying a large piece of pig fat which it dropped at Cuthbert's feet. He often thereafter told this story to visitors, producing the fat and offering to grease their boots to keep out the damp.

The fame of Cuthbert's wisdom and holiness spread throughout the land. The monks of Lindisfarne had many a story to tell their visitors about him. Soon many were visiting the island for advice, to make their confession and receive forgiveness, or to be healed of their sickness. Cuthbert seemed to see into the very heart of those who visited him. People came to him from all over the land with their troubles and no one seemed to go away without some relief and hope. But during all this time he was troubled by Boisil's prophecy that he would be made a bishop. He hoped it might not be so, and that he would be able to spend the rest of his life on Farne Island.

Another synod was held in the year 684, attended by king Ecgfrith and presided over by Archbishop Theodore. A bishop was needed and the name that came to the mind of them all was that of Cuthbert. Messengers and letters were sent, but he was reluctant to move. At last came the king and bishop Trumwine, accompanied by many other powerful and religious leaders. They knelt before Cuthbert and pleaded with him in the name of God to come with them. At last he consented, leaving for the synod with tears flowing down his face. Boisil's prophecy was coming true.

The intention had been to make Cuthbert bishop of Hexham, but it was finally agreed that Eata should be transferred to Hexham and Cuthbert appointed bishop of Lindisfarne. The winter of 684–5 he spent on Farne in prayer and solitude, preparing himself for his consecration.

At York on Easter Day, 685, Cuthbert's consecration took place. Archbishop Theodore presided and seven other bishops were present along with king Ecgfrith. Soon Ecgfrith and Theodore would be on the way to the consecration of St Paul's, Jarrow. As bishop, Cuthbert was given lands in York and a villa at Crayke where he could stay when he visited the city, but no doubt the man who wanted to be a hermit found all this deeply perturbing.

One of Cuthbert's earliest journeys as bishop was to Carlisle. It was 20 May, and he was being shown a Roman fountain and the walls of the city when suddenly he became deeply troubled. The people around him became still and wondered what was happening. Was the bishop ill? He leant on his staff, groaning as he looked sadly at the ground. At last he looked upwards and said in a low voice, 'Perhaps even now, at this very moment, the issue of the battle is decided.' Cuthbert was talking of king Ecgfrith; he had gone to do battle with the Picts, despite being warned by Cuthbert not to go.

A priest standing near Cuthbert asked him, 'How do you know?' Cuthbert replied, pointing to the sky, 'Do you not see how disturbed the elements are? There has been a sudden change. What mortal man is able to enquire into the deep things of God?'

It was Saturday. Leaving the city walls, Cuthbert went immediately to the queen and told her she must return to the royal city and fortress as soon as possible, in case the king had lost the battle and was killed. 'I would say go tomorrow but it is the Lord's day and it is not right for the queen to travel. I have a church to dedicate in the monastery tomorrow. Once this is done I will follow you and we will travel together to Bamburgh.' On the Monday, a soldier who had fled from the fight arrived to tell his sad tale: on the same day and at the same time that Cuthbert had become so distressed, the king had been laid low by a sword and all his bodyguard slain around him.

Not long after this, Cuthbert returned to Carlisle to ordain a number of priests and to clothe the queen herself in the monastic habit. While he was in the area, he was visited by a dear friend, Herbert. For a long time the two had been soul friends, each on their own island – Cuthbert on Farne Island and Herbert on a little island in Derwentwater – and for many years Herbert had travelled to Cuthbert for spiritual direction and teaching. At the end of their meeting Cuthbert said, 'Remember, brother Herbert, to ask me now for whatever you need, because after we have parted, we shall never again see one another in this world. For I am certain that the time of my departure is at hand.' When Herbert heard this he fell on his knees at Cuthbert's feet and with tears and sighs said: 'I beseech you in the name of the Lord not to leave me, but to remember your companion and ask the merciful God that as we have served him together on earth, so may we journey together towards the skies to see His glory.'

There was a long and deep silence while both men offered up their prayers and pleas to God. Then Cuthbert said: 'Rise up, brother, do not weep, because the clemency of Heaven has granted us what you have asked.' After this the men separated and did not see each other again in this world. Herbert had suffered from illness for a long while, and on the day of Cuthbert's death, he too died.

For two years Cuthbert went around caring for the people committed to his charge. He often taught by his own example;

even when busy he practised frugality and among the crowds preserved the rigours of monastic life. He gave food to the hungry, clothed the suffering, and wherever he went people said that miracles of healing happened. Two stories from this time illustrate vividly what often happened to bishop Cuthbert on his journeys.

Cuthbert was in the wild hill country between Hexham and Carlisle. When they heard he had arrived, the people from the outlying farms and homesteads gathered. There was no church in the area, not even a hut for the shelter of the bishop and his companion, so everyone made a shelter in the forest as best they could. Cuthbert remained there for two days, preaching and confirming the newly baptized. Suddenly a group of women appeared on the edge of the forest, carrying a young man who was wasting away with a grievous illness. Placing the youth down, they came to the bishop and asked that they might bring him to be blessed. Cuthbert agreed. When the youth was brought to him and Cuthbert saw his terrible affliction, he asked them all to move away. He began to pray, and after a period of deep silence he turned to look at the youth and gave him his blessing. The young man began to recover immediately; in the same hour he received food and was strengthened and gave thanks to God. He walked over to his friends who had been carrying him and they all returned to their homes.

At this time the plague was severe. It decimated villages, estates and monasteries: those that had once been crowded were left with only a small scattered remnant, and sometimes no one at all was left alive. Cuthbert travelled around seeking to bring relief and hope to these oppressed peoples. When preaching to the people of a village called Middleton, he asked, 'Is there anyone in the village still suffering from the pestilence, so that I may go and preach to him and bless him?' He was directed to a woman standing not far off, weeping and wailing on account that her son had recently died. She held another son in her arms. He was half dead, his body very swollen, and he was about to breathe his last. Cuthbert approached her and blessed the child. He said to the mother: 'Woman, do not weep; your son will be saved and no one of your household who is still alive will be harmed by the plague.' The mother and her son often testified to the truth of these words later in their lives.

Cuthbert had worked unceasingly for two years caring for his flock. He was now 52 years old, a good age for any man of his times, and especially because much of his life had been spent in austerity and he had suffered recurring troubles from earlier illnesses. He felt now that his travels would soon be over; he must resign from his episcopal oversight and prepare to meet his God. After the Christmas celebrations of 686 he resigned his see and left Lindisfarne for Farne Island and his hermitage. As the brethren watched the frail figure climb into the boat, one aged monk asked, 'Tell us, my lord bishop, when may we hope for your return.'

Aware that the end was near, Cuthbert replied, 'When you bring my body back here.' This caused a good deal of alarm among the brethren, but Cuthbert made little of it and set sail for Farne. He would not return to Lindisfarne alive.

Exercises

1 Though he wanted to be a hermit and spend his life in prayer, St Cuthbert never turned his back on the call of the community or of the individual that came to him. Think upon these words of Dietrich Bonhoeffer that relate to keeping a balanced life, and look at your own life to see if you are able to live this way: 'Let him who cannot be alone beware of community . . . Let him who is not in community beware of being alone . . . One who wants fellowship without solitude plunges into the

void of words and feelings, and one who seeks solitude without fellowship perishes in the abyss of vanity, self-infatuation and despair' (Bonhoeffer, 1952, pp. 77–8).

2 Our relationship with God is often dependent on our relationship with others. If we are insensitive to the needs of others it is not likely that we will be sensitive to God. A good guide is: 'Listen to others on behalf of God; listen to God on behalf of others. Go to God with others in your heart: go to others with God in your heart.' Remember that those who have the Good News of the gospel cannot keep this to themselves.

3 Read Luke 5.12–15.

Pause   Let your body and mind be rested. Breathe slowly and deeply. Check that your feet, your legs, your hands, your face, your neck are all relaxed. Let go of all tension. Encourage your mind to be still. It may help to picture a beautiful scene, but seek to still all wandering thoughts.

Presence   Rejoice in the presence and love of God. Know that God is with you. God never leaves you. Accept his love and offer your love to Him. Take your time: enjoy being relaxed in the presence. Affirm, 'You Lord are with me now and always. I know you love me.'

Picture   Visualize the leper and feel for his loneliness. Not only is his body diseased, he is an exile from his community. Leprosy is like living death. He has to keep his distance from others, calling out 'Unclean, unclean.' He cannot go home. He cannot be touched or hugged; he is in utter isolation, shunned and despised by society. Picture the man coming and throwing himself before Jesus, saying, 'Lord, if you are willing you can cleanse me.' Then see Jesus reach out and touch him. Jesus did not need to do that, but he saw that the man needed it; Jesus touched the untouchable and said, 'Be cleansed.' Through contact with Jesus this man's life is altered and he is made whole and wholesome.

Ponder   Think how Cuthbert also went out to the remote places and met the poor and neglected, how he cared for the outcast and the diseased. Do we see it as the role of the Church, our role, to reach out to the untouchables of society? Seek to know that God is not just concerned for our 'spirit' but for our whole being. God cares for our body, mind and spirit, and he wants us to be whole and wholesome. He also wants us in our well-being to reach out to those who are less fortunate than ourselves. Think about the neglected and the outcasts of our society and how the Saviour wants to touch them through us.

Promise   Promise that you will reach out to help those in need, that you may share in the saving work of Christ. Take to heart the words of Christ, 'Truly I tell you, just as you did it to one of the least of these who are members of my family, you did it to me' (Matthew 25.40). You may like to quietly read Matthew 25.31–46.

4 Pray:

> Good and gracious Lord,
> may I meet you in others,
> may I greet you in others
> may I know your love through others
> may I love you through others. Amen.

The last days

For two months Cuthbert was glad of the quiet and stillness of his hermitage, yet still people came for instruction and teaching. One day after his teaching was over Cuthbert said to the monks visiting him, 'I must return to my solitude, but before you go take some food. There is a goose hanging on the wall; cook it and eat it. Then you can board your vessel and return home.'

Cuthbert left for his cell, while the monks ate the food they had brought, but they left the goose as they had plenty of provisions. After their meal they were about to board their boat when a great storm arose, preventing them from sailing. For several days raging seas shut them in. All the time the goose hung on the wall. When they went to Cuthbert to complain about their delay, he merely asked them to be patient.

On the seventh day Cuthbert arrived at the guesthouse and warned the monks about the sins of disobedience. He had a twinkle in his eye when he said: 'Is the goose still hanging there uneaten? Did I not ask you to cook it and eat it? No wonder the sea is against you. Quickly, put it in the pot and cook it. Eat it, and then you will find that the sea is quiet again.'

They did as they were told and as soon as the goose was boiling in the pot, the wind eased and the waves lessened. After the meal they were able to get into their boat and sail away on a calm sea. Cuthbert smiled to himself. These young men might be learning to read books but they had not learnt to read the sea and the sky. Perhaps one day they would learn to be more sensitive. Even in his last days Cuthbert still had a sense of humour and fun.

Herefrith, the new abbot of Lindisfarne, was on Farne with some of the brethren. They stayed at the guesthouse and left Cuthbert on his own, though in fact some were trying to keep an eye on him at a distance. After they had been there three days, Herefrith approached Cuthbert's cell and gave the usual signal, desiring to receive a blessing. Cuthbert came to the window, but only gave a sigh. 'What is the matter, my lord bishop?' asked Herefrith. 'Has your old illness returned during the night?'

Cuthbert replied, 'Yes, illness has attacked me during the night.'

Herefrith assumed that it was another bout of the illness that had been bothering Cuthbert of late and asked for a blessing before he would leave for Lindisfarne. But Cuthbert's reply startled him. 'Do as you say. Get aboard your vessel and return home. Then, when God has taken my spirit, bury me in this dwelling near my oratory towards the south, on the eastern side of the cross I have erected there. I have hidden a sarcophagus, which abbot Cudda once gave me, under the turf on the north side of the oratory. Place my body in this and wrap my body up in the cloth you will find there. I was unwilling to wear this cloth while alive but out of love for the abbess Verca, who gave it to me, I have kept it for this very purpose.'

Herefrith was deeply concerned for Cuthbert and asked that some of the brethren should be allowed to remain on the island, but Cuthbert was firmly against this. 'No. Go now and when you come again God will direct you.' Herefrith pleaded in vain. It was very obvious that Cuthbert wanted to be left on his own. Once back on Lindisfarne, Herefrith called all the brothers together to pray for Cuthbert, 'for it seems that his time for departure is near at hand.'

For the next five days storms raged and the seas were heavy. No one was able to cross to the Farne and attend to Cuthbert. When the storm ceased, Herefrith and some of the brethren took a boat and set sail. On their arrival they found that Cuthbert was not in his own dwelling but in the guesthouse, weary from lack of food and the effects of his distressing illness; his foot was swollen and an ulcer needed attention. The brethren left Herefrith on the island with Cuthbert and returned to Lindisfarne. Herefrith gently washed Cuthbert's feet before persuading him to take a little heated wine. Throughout this time Cuthbert remained silent. Herefrith, not sure of what to say, said, 'I see, my lord bishop, that you have been severely ill since we left. You should have let one of us stay.'

In a very frail voice Cuthbert replied: 'As soon as you left, my illness became much worse. I came to this place so that when you arrived you would find me here and not need to enter my dwelling. I have been in this place for five days and nights without moving.'

'But how could you survive without food?' asked Herefrith. In answer Cuthbert drew back the coverlet on the bed to reveal five onions. 'This has been my food whenever I was hungry.' But Herefrith noticed that only one onion showed any signs of being nibbled at. Then in a vigorous voice Cuthbert said: 'This has been a great time of battling against the old enemy. I have fought the fight and finished the course.'

Herefrith spoke gently to Cuthbert, telling him that if he was to stay on the island he must have someone to look after him. Cuthbert agreed: he did not want to have to leave Farne but to die there. And so, from that day he had someone to care for him. On his return to Lindisfarne, Herefrith told the brethren how ill Cuthbert was and that he wanted to be buried on Farne. 'But I think it is more fitting that we persuade him to bring his body here and bury it with due honours in the church.' And all of the community agreed that it would be good for Cuthbert to be buried on Lindisfarne.

On his next visit Herefrith made a cautious approach to Cuthbert. 'We did not dare, my lord bishop, to disobey your command to bury you here, but we ask you to count us worthy of the honour of your presence in death. We would like you to be buried on Lindisfarne as befits a bishop.'

Cuthbert looked at Herefrith with sorrow in his eyes. 'It was my deep desire to rest here, where I have fought the fight for the Lord and from where I had hoped to rise in glory. It would be better for you if I were to remain here. I see that fugitives and guilty men will seek sanctuary where I lie. You will have difficulties with the powers of this world if you allow this to happen. The presence of my body may cause you much trouble and disturbance in the future.' He could see that Herefrith was not convinced and that his request grieved the brethren, so he continued, 'If you wish to take me away from here, it would be better if you bury me in the interior of the church. Then you can have some control over who can come in or not.' At this Herefrith was delighted, but he failed to see the sorrow in the old man's eyes.

Cuthbert then requested that he be carried back to his oratory. Four of the brethren did this with great care. Until now no one had been allowed to enter his own dwelling. Now Cuthbert was persuaded to let one monk enter and to stay with him; he looked about him and chose. 'Let Walhstod enter with me.' For a long time this brother too had suffered from illness, but after being with Cuthbert for six hours he declared that he had been healed, and time proved this to be true. Cuthbert however declared that if he had any power in this matter, surely he would have healed himself. He did not want credited to him any powers that were God's alone.

Soon after this, Walhstod entered the oratory to find Cuthbert lying in a corner opposite the altar where he had often worshipped. Cuthbert had great difficulty in speaking, but managed to say a few words about the need for peace and humility among the brethren and the danger of those who fought against these things. He said psalms and prayed continually. At the accustomed time of nightly prayer he received his communion for the last time on earth. Then, lifting his hands in praise, he departed to the Father.

Immediately Walhstod rushed out to tell the brethren, who were spending the night in a vigil of prayer. At that moment they were singing Psalm 60, which begins: 'O God you have cast us off and broken us; you have been angry; restore us to yourself again . . . That your beloved may be delivered, save us by your right hand and answer us.'

One of the monks went outside. Lighting two torches, he waved them in his hands, giving the agreed signal to let the monks of Lindisfarne know that Cuthbert had passed into life eternal. When the brother keeping watch on Lindisfarne saw the pinpricks of light, he thought at first that his eyes were deceiving him. Then he made the sign of the cross towards Farne – his own blessing of Cuthbert – and ran to the church, where the same service was being said. The monks continued the psalm, well aware that the watcher had entered. When he arrived they were saying exactly the same words: 'O God you have cast us off and broken us . . .'

The psalm seemed to be full of foreboding, and as events were to unfold in the following months it seemed as if its words were being fulfilled. There was a whole year of troubles; only when Eadbert was consecrated as bishop did the storms cease and the latter part of the psalm find its fulfilment: 'Through God will we do great acts, for it is he that shall tread down our enemies.'

A boat was sent to Farne to bring Cuthbert's body back for burial, and upon its return to Lindisfarne it was met by a great crowd of people. A grave had been prepared in the church of St Peter at the right hand side of the altar and the stone sarcophagus awaited Cuthbert. He was wrapped in the fine linen cloth that abbess Verca had given to him and dressed in his priestly vestments with shoes on his feet, while an unconsecrated host was laid on his breast. His soul was commended to his Maker whom he knew so well, to his Saviour whom he served faithfully, and to the Spirit who had filled him from the beginning. Each of the brethren in turn threw a handful of soil on to the coffin and signed him with the cross. The holy man was now with the angels who had often been his companions. He had completed his pilgrimage and this was his birth day in the fullness of God's heavenly kingdom.

The story of Cuthbert's life is over but his adventures in death are yet another story. After his death miracles were recorded at his tomb on Lindisfarne and people came in great numbers to his grave. Eleven years after his death on 20 March 687, it was decided to elevate his body: that is, dig up his mortal remains, wash the bones and place them where they might be seen and venerated. To everyone's surprise, when the sarcophagus was opened they found Cuthbert's body still intact; he looked as if he was just sleeping. Cuthbert's body was washed, given new clothing and then elevated within the church for people to see. Cuthbert's shrine became one of the most visited shrines in Europe and one of the richest. This continued until the Viking invasion in 793 when the church was plundered, though Cuthbert's shrine remained intact.

Due to other Viking invasions along the coast over the next few years the monks decided to leave Lindisfarne and to take Cuthbert's body, along with Oswald's head and Aidan's relics, to a safer place. At first they moved just a little way inland to Norham on the river Tweed. A fiercer round of invasions, which included the destruction of the monasteries at Tynemouth, Wearmouth and Jarrow, caused the monks to leave Norham.

The last days

Over the next few years, the monks travelled all over the north of England evading capture until times became more settled, when they made their home at Chester-le-Street. A fine new church was built and it was soon endowed with many gifts. In 934 the grandson of Alfred the Great, king Athelstan, visited the shrine bearing gifts of silver and gold, valuable vestments and a copy of Bede's *Life of Cuthbert*.

The following years were good ones for the monks looking after Cuthbert's body, but in 995 there was another Viking uprising and they were on the move once more. The monks, who were affectionately called 'Cuthbert's folk', went to Ripon where they stayed for four months. After this they decided to return north.

Legend tells us that as they came close to Chester-le-Street, the wagon carrying Cuthbert's coffin became stuck in the mud. After vain attempts to move it the monks decided it was a sign they should go elsewhere with the relics. One monk had heard a voice saying, 'Take the body of the saint to Dunholm', but no one knew where it was. Just at that moment two women passed near. One said, 'I have lost my red cow with the short horns. Have you seen her?' 'Yes,' replied the other, 'I saw her not long ago at Dunholm.' When the monks heard this they were overjoyed and asked to be guided to Dunholm, and to their wonder they found that the cart carrying the coffin had come strangely free from the mud. They proceeded to Dunholm, or Durham, and built there a church as a shrine for Cuthbert's remains. A carving of the woman with a cow can be seen on the outside of the cathedral on its north wall.

At least, that is the legend. More likely, the community that cared for Cuthbert had grown to such a size that they needed a larger home and chose Durham because of its situation on the river Wear. A temporary church of wood was built to house the relics as well as for worship. By 999 a stone Saxon church was ready and Cuthbert's relics were translated into it.

On 11 August 1093 the foundation stones of the present cathedral were laid, and by 1104 the building was sufficiently complete for Cuthbert's coffin to be translated into the apse. Immediately before this the monks inspected Cuthbert's body and saw that it remained incorrupt. Cuthbert's body remained in the shrine until its dismantling at the Reformation. Eventually the relics were buried under the original site of the shrine.

In 1827 the bones were re-examined and then reburied. The secondary relics, such as the vestments, the pectoral cross, the portable altar and the contemporary coffin, were removed and are now on display in the cathedral.

Cuthbert is remembered on 20 March, the day he died. But because this day always falls in Lent, many keep 4 September, the day of his translation into the cathedral, as his main festival. Let us too rejoice in the life of the holy man of God, one of the strange ones who lived in Northumbria.

Exercises

1 Think about the saying, 'Whoever is afraid of death is afraid to adventure and so is afraid to live.' To talk of death is often a forbidden subject because it is seen as the end of all things. Christians must see it as the gate to the fullness of life eternal and as their 'birth day'. Here are some words written by Athanasius of Alexandria in the fourth century:

> Death is a pilgrimage, a lifetime's pilgrimage which none of us must shirk. It is a pilgrimage from decay to imperishable life, from mortality to immortality, from anxiety to tranquillity of mind. Do not be afraid of the word death: rather rejoice in the

blessings which follow a happy death. After all what is death
but the burial of sin and the harvest of goodness.

(Athanasius, *On the Blessing of Death*, 4, 15,
quoted in Atwell, 2004, p. iii)

2 Read 1 Corinthians 15.35–44, 50–54.

Pause   Stop all that you are doing. Let your body have a break
and relax. I have discovered that relaxed people usually achieve
far more; too much tension can be destructive. Check each part
of your body and see that it is relaxed. If you find an area that
is tense, seek to relax it. Little pauses like these throughout the
day are beneficial to well-being. Let your mind too relax, seek
to be rid of anxieties by visualizing calm and beautiful scenes.
Get your body and mind to be as still as possible.

Presence   Rejoice in the presence of God the giver of life.
Know that God is with you and gives you life and love. Let his
presence renew and refresh you: allow God to give you new
courage and strength.

Picture   Imagine seed being buried in the ground and 'dying'
away. It would be easy to think it is gone for ever. Now watch
as the first shoots appear. That which was buried is rising. It
looks quite different from the grain, and yet we know it is linked
with it. If oats were buried it will be oats that rise, if barley then
it will be barley. There is death, burial, destruction, and yet what
rises is of the seed and is the same grain, though different. Here
is a wonderful mystery. Now think how you are such a mystery. Look at a photograph album of yourself, images of you as
a baby, an infant, a junior, a teenager, a young adult and so on.
Already God has given you many bodies – and yet all are you
and in a way the same body. About every seven years your body

has died away and been renewed. Though your earthly bodies die away, you are still renewed – and so it is with what we call death. You may be dissolved by death, you may be changed by the resurrection, but it is still you who exists and survives.

Ponder   The reality for us, through the resurrection of Jesus Christ, is that death is not the end but rather the 'great adventure'. As I like to tell people, 'Death is not fatal'! Read verses 53–54 and affirm them as a truth that relates to you: 'For this perishable body must put on imperishability and this mortal body must put on immortality. When this perishable body puts on imperishability and this mortal body puts on immortality, then the saying that is written will be fulfilled: "Death has been swallowed up in victory".' Know that you arise today in the power of God, that in his love you arise from death.

Promise   Promise that you will affirm the saving power of God by giving thanks each day for the resurrection of the body. Let him help you to enjoy life to the full and to know that life is eternal.

3 Rejoice in the lives of Aidan, Bede and Cuthbert. Give thanks for their faith, for their witness and influence and that they are in the fullness of life eternal. Affirm that faith in these words of Augustine of Hippo:

> All shall be Amen and Alleluia.
> We shall rest and we shall see,
> We shall see and we shall know,
> We shall know and we shall love,
> We shall love and we shall praise.
> Behold our end which is no end.

Bibliography

David Adam, *The Edge of Glory*, London: SPCK 1997

David Adam, *Fire of the North: The Illustrated Life of Cuthbert*, London: SPCK 1993

David Adam, *Flame in my Heart: St Aidan for Today*, London: Triangle 1997

Anon, *Life of Ceolfrith*, trans. D. S. Boutflower, London 1912

Robert Atwell, *Celebrating the Saints*, London: SCM Press 2004

Bedae Historia Ecclesiastica Gentis Anglorum: Venerabilis Bedae Opera Historica, Vol. 1, ed. C. Plummer, Oxford 1896

Bede, *A History of the English Church and People*, trans. Leo Sherley-Price, London: Penguin 1968

Peter Hunter Blair, *The World of Bede*, Cambridge: Cambridge University Press 1970

Peter Hunter Blair, *Northumbria in the Days of Bede*, Llanerch Publishers 1996

Dietrich Benhoeffer, *Life Together*, New York: Harper & Row 1952

Bertram Colgrave (ed.), *Two Lives of Saint Cuthbert*, Cambridge: Cambridge University Press 1985

Rosemary Cramp, *The Background of Cuthbert's Life*, Durham: Durham Cathedral Lecture 1980

D. H. Farmer (ed.), *The Age of Bede*, London: Penguin 1983

Alfred C. Fryer, *Aidan Apostle of England*, S. W. Partridge 1902

John Marsden, *The Illustrated Bede*, London: Guild Publishing 1989

John Marsden, *Northanhymbre Saga*, London: Kyle Cathie 1992

D. W. Rollason (ed.), *Cuthbert Saint and Patron*, Dean and Chapter of Durham 1987

C. J. Stranks, *The Life and Death of St Cuthbert*, London: SPCK 1964

Benedicta Ward, *The Venerable Bede*, London: Geoffrey Chapman 1998